D1283792

Are
You
Talking
To
Me?

DON COREY

Outskirts Press, Inc.
Denver, Colorado

Acknowledgements

To my lovely wife, Katherine, who endured numerous copy rewrites and title changes, yet never lost her affable demeanor.

To Mars Eghigian and Janice Denham, who helped to ensure the words I chose were actual words.

To Jean Spezia, admittedly my biggest fan, even though I have no idea why I deserve such an honor.

Finally, to my loyal fans: Dave Warner, Barbara Moresi, Jim Bleikamp, Brenda Switzer, Dave Horstmann, Debbie Sheil, Bill Yenecek, Shannon Kelly, Doug Bankston, Penelope Cox, Terry Moses, Jeanie Pfaff, Joe Babcock, Sharon Lockart, Joel Clayton, Laura Leech, Jerry Boyle, Richard Herman, Bob Macheska, Paul Mandel, Bob Sparks, Jim Larsen, Butch Basemore, Thom Price, Mark Newport, Michael Yaffe, Bob Eddings, John Dewey, John Neiman, the guys at the "Frigid Meat Company," Paul, the "tow truck guy," and numerous other nameless voices in the night, who helped to make radio broadcasting the most fun occupation I ever had.

ONE

ost people go through their whole life without doing what they really want to do. I was fortunate. I discovered my passion early, chased it and made it mine. But there were surprises I did not anticipate.

Much that happens later in life depends upon how your life starts out. I always knew I was a little different from all the other kids...but at first I wasn't sure why. That would come later; I wish it had been a lot later. I was born prematurely. If I had known what kind of lunacy was waiting for me "out there," I'd have stayed in much longer. They would've had to pull me out with those "salad tongs." But no, I had to come out and see what was going on.

I started out scrawny and pretty much stayed that way for a very long time. My poor dad; he was handsome and athletic. He played baseball, football

Don Corey

-- you name it he played it. And he played it well. As for me, I couldn't walk across a field without falling and hurting myself. I was always the last one picked in sports. Actually, that's not quite true. I was *never picked at all*; I was the one at the end, after everyone else had been chosen. The one where they'd say, "Great -- we got Don, there goes the game!" Don't think that this is sad, oh no. This is exactly what taught me how to have a sense of humor, the thing that has carried me through life, the very thing that people who know me like most about me.

For example, when I was attending grade school at Edgar Road Elementary, we were all supposed to come to class dressed up as something for Halloween. My grandma, a designer for a fabric company, was quite skilled at making dresses, skirts, jackets -- she could make almost anything. She designed me an odd-looking costume. It was supposed to be a "hot dog." It actually did look like a hot dog nestled inside a bun -- like the walking and talking hot dog that used to be seen on those drive-in movie promos. When suited-up in this contraption, only my feet would stick out and my head resided inside the suit. There was just a very thin mesh in the front to enable me to see out. It zipped up the back, so once it was in place, my arms would be on the inside. I could do little else except walk in a straight line and try not to bump into anything.

My great grandma Minnie, a strong and tough German woman, helped me into this costume and zippered me up. It was an overcast day, cloudy and gloomy, but I was in high spirits because I couldn't wait to show off my unique outfit. Surely no one else

2

would be thusly attired.

I walked about four blocks to the school. I was running a little late in my attempts to not fall down, but as I started up the steep hill leading to the school, I could tell there was trouble ahead. There, near the top of the hill, were two older kids -- probably teenagers I thought. They wore black leather jackets and smoked cigarettes. As I approached, I heard one say to the other, "Hey, check out the dude in the hot-dog suit."

I was sure this was not good, but there was really nowhere else to go. I was already late and was sure I would not be able to outrun these hoodlums. It was all I could manage just to walk in this get-up, much less run. So I plodded forward timidly, waiting for what would happen next. I did not have long to wait. The other kid said to his fellow hooligan, "Let's have a little fun with him." The two of them started to push me back and forth between them. I maintained my balance as long as I could, not speaking to them at all, just hoping and praying I could just "get through this." The one kid gave me one final shove, as the other stepped aside. I fell to the ground with a sickening thud that momentarily knocked the wind out of me. Then the two of them together gave me a shove and I started to roll down the hill. They kept after me until I reached the bottom and landed against a wire fence. At this point, they figured they'd had enough fun and ran away laughing hysterically.

At first I was relieved. After all, I wasn't hurt. Not physically anyway. My pride was probably ruined at this point, but I didn't care so much about that. What

3

Don Corey

I did care about was, with my arms and legs inside this stupid costume, I was not able to stand up. I rolled around for several minutes and just could not right myself. I finally figured out that if I turned just slightly, I could push with my feet and gradually inch my back up the wire fence. At last I was on my feet again and headed back up the steep hill. I hoped these guys had really run off. If they had been at the top of the hill, I wasn't sure I could go through it again.

Thankfully, they were gone. When I finally got to class I thought my troubles were over, but the teacher wanted to know, "Why were you late?" I was going to explain that I had met up with some bullies -- but I just didn't want to relive the whole thing again. I could tell by this little adventure that I was going to have to live my life by using my wits.

TWO

The question now was: Where could I get some wits?

As a kid, I pretty much kept to myself. I had an active imagination and considered myself something of an inventor. For example, I really admired Thomas Edison and Benjamin Franklin. They came up with some pretty awesome stuff, but I was hard- pressed to do anything that great. Not that I didn't try.

My dad kept a Big Ben alarm clock on his workbench in the garage. It had a very loud bell that for some reason I found fascinating. I would listen to the tick-tick-ticking sound and watch the second hand moving with each tick, I wondered, what in the world is going on in there?

So I borrowed some of dad's tools, and took the clock to my room for a little bit of surgery. Incidentally, these would be the same tools I would later leave out in the back yard until they became rusty and useless, thereby giving my dad another opportunity to practice "anger management."

I had never disassembled anything. But I thought, how hard can it be? You take something out, you remember where it came from, and you put it back. Simple enough. I don't remember how many screws I had to remove to take the back of the clock off -- but I'll never forget the result. As I carefully removed the back, it suddenly lurched and a large, tightly coiled spring flew at me. It made an odd noise like "Zing!" as it flew by, nearly slicing off the tip of my index finger. I could not believe such a huge spring could fit into such a small space. Those Swiss clock makers must really be something, to get that big old spring in that little case. I tried unsuccessfully for hours to put in back. My first surgery was a failure. Now I knew what made it tick, but it would never tick again. I had to go to my father and say, "Dad, you know that clock with the loud alarm? It won't be loud anymore."

Thankfully, although dad was aggravated, he didn't get all that mad. Oh, there would be plenty of that later. This little operation, I knew, was just the beginning. Yes, there was much more that had to be done. But I would have to "lay low" for a while.

Advertisements in the back of comic books fascinated me. There were always interesting items to be had if you didn't mind spending a few weeks worth of allowance money and then waiting six to eight weeks for it to arrive by mail. I instinctively knew the "X-Ray Specs" had to be a sham. I mean, come on -- glasses that would allow you to see what was under someone's clothes? No way could that be possible, or even legal. What did catch my eye was an ad for a "Giant Weather Balloon." Now this looked interesting indeed. It had a picture of the balloon with a man standing next to it, dwarfed in comparison. This was one huge balloon! I immediately sent off my money and prepared for the eight-week agony of watching the mailbox.

I will never forget the day it arrived. The package itself was huge, but the big surprise was the immensity of the neatly folded balloon itself. Unfolded, it was almost as big as a bed sheet. It had a nozzle at the end that was as big around as a soda bottle bottom. Of course, I was delighted that it was as big as the ad had promised, but how in the world was I supposed to inflate it? Even if I could do it with just lungpower, it would take a week.

Then an idea hit me. My parents and grandparents had left to eat lunch using my parents' car. That meant my Grandpa's station wagon was parked in the driveway. He kept the keys in his top dresser drawer. I grabbed the keys and ran outside with the balloon. My idea was to put the nozzle end of the balloon over the tail pipe of the car and then use the exhaust fumes to inflate it. I placed a large rubber band over the nozzle to secure it to the tail pipe. Once I was sure it was properly fastened, I hopped in and started up the car. As soon as the car was running, I got out to make sure the balloon was filling up properly and not getting pinched. It worked perfectly. Within minutes, the balloon was so huge it completely obscured the back of the car. Excited, I thought, "The guys will never believe this!" I jumped back into the car and turned off the ignition. I got down on the ground to remove the balloon from its moorings.

A small flaw appeared in my plan. The hot exhaust pipe had melted the nozzle of the balloon and it would not pull free. I tried to gently pull it, but it would not budge. For a moment I felt a little panicky. It wouldn't look good if my parents and grandparents pulled up and saw this giant monstrosity attached to the family car. Then another idea came to me. I raced inside and got a razor blade. I knelt under the car and gingerly started to cut away at the back end of the nozzle, being careful not to puncture the balloon itself. I also had to make sure the giant rubber band stayed on the end, or the balloon would just fly backwards all over the neighborhood and I'd be right back where I started. After a few minutes of gently sawing away, the balloon was almost free of the pipe. I gave it one last gentle tug and it popped free!

As it did, it knocked me backwards and I quickly became airborne. I should have seen this coming, but I completely forgot that the exhaust fumes were hot! It was moving fast and there was no way I could grab it. I quickly jumped on my bike and started off down the street. If I could just keep it in sight, maybe the hot gasses would cool and it would come down. It hovered aloft about 15 to 20 feet and moved pretty quickly. I chased it for two or three blocks, and then it suddenly lodged itself in a tall tree. "This is good," I thought, glad that it had stopped. Just then a breeze blew and the tree branches started to sway. "Now It'll come down." I said to myself. Unfortunately it was not to be. The branches of the tree pierced the skin of the balloon, which loudly exploded as the hot gasses flew out. My giant weather balloon, looking so impressive only moments before, was now just a big white hunk of vinyl hanging and swinging in the breeze. Six weeks' worth of allowance money and eight weeks of waiting had culminated in 10 minutes worth of excitement, followed by bitter disappointment. I was right about one thing though – "the guys will never believe this."

THREE

I have always been gullible. I'm getting a little better in my old age, but not much. When a young lad this sometimes got me into tight situations. Like the time my friend Steve and I decided our "allowance money" just wasn't taking us as far as we would have liked. We weren't really into the "mowing the lawn" thing that most kids our age did to earn some extra cash. We considered that a little too strenuous, thank you. So Steve hit on what he considered a brilliant idea. It was summertime in St. Louis and hot as blazes. Steve said, "Let's wash cars!"

Yes, we could go all around the neighborhood with a bucket and some soap and charge a dollar a car. Of course, any business should have equipment and capital for start-up expenses. We had none of that. We did scrounge around and come up with an old bucket and some sponges and rags, but we didn't have money to buy Turtle Wax. "No problem," said

Don Corey

Steve- "we've got some laundry detergent downstairs at my house." I asked, "Are you sure you can use laundry detergent on a car?" Steve said, "Hey, soap is soap." That certainly sounded logical, so off we went. Up and down the block, knocking on doors and trying to get someone interested in having his car washed. This was a lot more difficult than I thought it would be. I was the guy giving the sales pitch to the homeowner, while Steve stayed just out of sight where only I could see him. He would say funny things "off camera" to try to get me to laugh. This was just what I needed, a distraction to make the sale even harder.

At one house, a woman answered the doorbell. She only opened the big wooden door and looked at me through the screen door. I tried to begin my sales pitch, but she was perturbed about something. She held back a vicious-looking dog that growled and tried to lunge at me through the screen. I started to say, "Would you like your car washed?" She cut me off mid sentence- saying, "Shh -- the baby's sleeping." Steve, hearing this statement from his little hiding spot whispers so only I could hear, "What's that got to do with washing a car?" The door shuts in my face and it's time to go to the next house. After several hours of walking around in the hot sun with our bucket in hand, we decide it's just not working out. My dad was in the front yard. We told him the whole story. He told us we could wash his car and he'd give us the dollar. Finally we had a paying customer. We got out the hose, filled the bucket and added the detergent. We washed the whole car and decided we'd done a fine job. We collected our dollar and went to take a break and drink a soda.

Are You Talking To Me?

Ten minutes later the sound of my dad yelling for us pierced the neighborhood. We ran to see what the excitement was all about. Dad's car had dried and it was a mess! It was streaked with white and nasty looking. Dad said, "What in the world did you wash the car with?" We said, "Uh...laundry detergent." Dad immediately gave us some more money and told us to go buy some real detergent and wash the car right. We did just that and it turned out all right. But Steve and I thought, what if we *had* washed the whole block's cars? Man, they would've been after us like the crowds carrying torches and out for blood in those old Frankenstein movies!

When my dad was a young boy, walking home from school one day, he found an odd- looking cylindrical object and decided to carry it with him as he walked. He would throw it in the air and run and catch it. He did this over and over until he finally reached home. As soon as he came in the door, his mother yelled out, "You're late. Wash your hands and come to the dinner table."

Dad still had the cylindrical tube in his hand and he laid it aside next to the stove and went to wash his hands. He then joined the family at the dinner table.

He did not know the object he had brought home was meant to be used in an automobile as a prank. It would be mounted to the engine of a car. When the engine got hot enough, it would throw off sparks and smoke, to make the unknowing victim think there was something wrong with his engine.

After the device sat next to the stove for a while, it

got hot enough to ignite. Since it was not bolted to an engine, it took off and became airborne. It came flying into the living room where it flew over everyone's head, with a shower of sparks and smoke. It then made a loud whistling sound and exploded! Dad's mom passed out.

When Dad told me this story, I silently breathed a sigh of relief. I knew then that no matter what kind of bizarre circumstances I might wander into, none could possibly top this little mishap. It's always handy to know something your parents' did- that is equal to, or worse than anything you've done or plan to do. I call this, "children-inadvertent mishap-insurance."

Another funny thing that dad stumbled into innocently happened when I was about 12. While shopping he picked up an expensive can of Macadamia nuts to surprise my mom. He came back to where he thought he had parked. There was another car that looked exactly like his. The same make and model, even the same color. He inserted the key into the door and it opened right up. He hopped in and put the nuts on the passenger seat. But when he tried to start the car, the key would not turn. Suddenly, he saw he was *in the wrong car!* Afraid that someone would think he was stealing it, he leaped out and locked the door behind him. He stepped quickly onto the sidewalk and saw his car just two spaces away. Still nervous, he jumped in and sped away.

It wasn't until he got home that he realized he'd left the nuts in that car. We laughed out loud thinking about that guy – asking himself -- why would nuts appear in a locked car? What sort of burglar doesn't take anything, leaves a gift, and then locks up afterwards?

My dad's name was Duane. He was a great role model to me. He was an honest man. You've always heard the stories about Abraham Lincoln who would walk miles to return a book or some such thing. This may or may not have been true of old Abe, but it was true of my Dad. He would go miles out of his way to repay a debt, to right a wrong. He always brought me up to believe that not only was honesty the best policy, it should be the only policy. He always told me that no matter what I did, no matter how bad, it was better to tell the truth and take the punishment than lie and end up the worst for it.

Dad was also very frugal. I once brought home a girlfriend for my dad to meet. She said to him, "Can't you do something about your son? He's so cheap." I replied, "I'm not cheap...I'm frugal." Dad looked her straight in the eye, winked, and said, "He's not frugal -- he's cheap."

He was honest to a fault, but at the same time his eyes would flash with anger when he perceived arrogance. With righteous indignation he would come down on you like a sack of bricks if that's what he felt was needed. One of his jobs required him to deposit money at the local bank. He handed the bank clerk the money and the clerk handed him the change he was supposed to have coming. Dad quickly looked at it and realized they had given him an extra $10.00 in error. So, of course, my dad said to the man, "Excuse me sir, you made a mistake." The man gave my dad a look of disgust and replied, "We don't make mistakes here." My surprised dad said, "Really? Can I borrow that pencil there?" He pointed to the pencil on the counter. The clerk handed it to him. He bit the eraser off and flipped it at the clerk and said, "You won't be needing that!" Then he walked out.

Always careful about spending money, he would sometimes frequent garage and yard sales to get something at a great discount. One time he had bought a belt at a yard sale. He was so happy about this "handsome-looking belt" that he had gotten for almost nothing. I had heard him talk about it, but I had never seen it. Finally he said, "You know, every time I wear this belt I get all kinds of compliments on it from the people I ride with on the bus. And these are young kids, they always say, 'Man, I love that belt.'" So I asked to see this belt that these people liked so much. When he brought it out, I started laughing. Dad said, "What?" I said, "Do you know what that is on that belt buckle?" Dad said, "Sure, it's a big leaf." I said, "Dad, that's a giant marijuana leaf!" He never wore it again.

Dad also had a peculiar sense of humor. When I was about nine years old, I came in from playing in the yard. Dad was on the couch reading. As I walked by, he said, "Hey Don, you want to see a magic trick?" I said, "Sure." So he said, "I'm going to clean up this entire living room without getting off the couch." Well, that sounded pretty impressive to me so I said, "Yeah, I'd like to see that." So Dad said, "O.K. now before I do that, take this empty soda bottle and put it in the kitchen." So I took the bottle into the kitchen and quickly ran back to dad and said, "O.K. I'm ready."

So then he said, "Put this stack of papers over there on the coffee table." So I did that, wishing he'd hurry up, quit handing me this stuff and get on with the magic. Then he said, "Now take this plate and put it in the kitchen sink." It was on my way to the kitchen for the second time that it dawned on me where this "magic trick" was going. As I came back into the living room again, I smiled knowingly at Dad and he smiled back. "That's real cute, Dad," I said. That would be my first experience with what I would later learn as delegating.

He taught me other important lessons about life. Once while we watched a show on television, he said, "What do you think of Jimmy Durante?" I replied, "I think he's great." Dad said, "Really? I always thought he was kind of a jerk." I was really surprised to hear him say that. I really liked him. I said, "Well, I think he's neat." Dad smiled real big and I could tell he was up to something. When I asked him he said, "I just said that to see what you'd say. You see, Donald, some kids will just say what they think their parents want to hear. When I said I didn't like that guy, most kids your age will change their mind and say they don't like them either. You stuck with what you believed and that's good."

These were the kind of lessons that meant a lot to me and they've stayed with me through my adult life. One time I had done something wrong; something serious enough that dad decided warranted a spanking. He only spanked me a few times and it was only for serious infractions. He never used a belt, only his bare hand. And he never did it out of anger. In fact, he would explain why I was receiving the

Don Corey

punishment before he did it, so I would understand the lesson I was to learn. He was always extremely fair. This particular time though, I felt the spanking was more than I deserved. As I sat in my room crying afterwards, I remembered something. Dad always said if there was anything bothering me, I could talk to him about it, no matter how serious. So I decided to tell him I thought this judgment was unfair.

I knew I was taking a chance and I might just end up with another spanking, but I decided to try anyway. I went to dad and explained that I felt that this discipline was more than I deserved and that the punishment didn't fit the crime. Dad looked me straight in the eye and said, "So that's what you think?" My knees got a little shaky and I thought, "Oh, no -- here it comes." Dad smiled and said, "Well, you are absolutely right. I was upset over something else that happened today and I mistakenly took it out on you. I'm very sorry and I hope you'll forgive me."

What a relief that was! I grinned and said, "Oh, that's ok." It was a moment I will never forget. It takes a big man to admit when he is wrong and my dad was that big man. I always hoped someday I could do as well.

Me and Dad

FOUR

At about the age of 10 I started to listen to the radio. I had a small transistor set that my grandma had given me for my birthday. It was pretty small, about the size of a deck of playing cards. I plugged a little earphone into it, and listened in my bed when my parents thought I was asleep. I could hardly believe all the different things I could hear with this tiny little device. I could listen to one station for a while and then turn the tuning dial and get another completely different set of sounds. I still am fascinated today. How much information is flying around out there invisible, in the air and all you need is the right equipment and you can tune it right in. I started around 1959 or so, listening randomly at first, just seeing "what was out there," but at some point I ended up at 1430 on the dial, which was, at the time, WIL. I stayed at that spot for some time because, not only did they play the music I liked the best, but their announcers seemed really happy and friendly. I wasn't sure at the time why this made such a difference to me, but I guess it was just fun.

Unfortunately, one day I left my cherished radio out in the back yard and during the night it rained. It wasn't a light shower either, it poured. When I discovered my mistake, I was mortified! I figured it was probably shot and would have to be thrown out. "When Grandma finds out what I did, she probably won't even buy me another one. " I'd be afraid to even ask her. Luckily, I had a plan. I let the excess water pour out while I held it upside down and at an angle. Then I placed it on the sunny windowsill in my room. I waited about three days for it to dry out, and then put in a new battery and turned it on. It actually still worked! However, I could never get WIL again. Something must have rusted at that spot on the tuning mechanism, but at least all the other stations came in just fine. So I simply tuned around the dial until I found another station that was playing the same kind of music that I had liked on WIL. That station turned out to be KXOK.

I told my friend Dave about this station and we both started to listen to it a lot. The DJs always mentioned that they were at "Radio Park." Dave and I weren't quite sure what that meant, but we did know they were located at 1600 North Kingshighway in St. Louis.

One day in the middle of the afternoon we were listening to KXOK and we heard the DJ say, "It's dark here at Radio Park." Dave and I asked each other in amazement, "It's only three o'clock in the afternoon. How can it be dark there? Is there a storm or something?"

Are You Talking To Me?

We came to find out that the DJ on the air was Danny Dark. That was just a little catch phrase he used on his show.

My friend Dave was like a brother to me. But he did have one little quirk that used to drive me crazy. When he came to our house, he would head right for the cookie jar and take some without asking. I told him, "Look, Dave, I don't mind you having a few cookies, but it would be nice if you would ask first." This request was ignored. Each time he came over, he'd do the same thing again. I decided to hatch up a plan to break him of this annoying habit.

I knew he'd be coming over again Saturday. There were still three Oreo cookies left. I took them from the jar and pulled them apart. I gently scraped off the white icing and went in search for a nasty-tasting, but non-poisonous, substitute.

I decided to use a hair crème for men. It came in a tube, like toothpaste. It was the same white color as the icing, with the same consistency. This would taste awful enough to prove my point, but non-toxic enough to do no harm. I painstakingly reassembled them, making sure they looked perfect and not tampered with. I chuckled to myself as I pictured how hilarious this would be, if I could just pull it off.

I placed the altered goodies into the jar. Within minutes, the knock at the door signaled that the moment had arrived. As I headed for the door I thought, maybe he won't even go for it and I'll have wasted my last three delicacies. But Dave came in and headed straight for the goods. This is it, I thought.

Don Corey

This is going to be great! He opened the lid and took out his snack. Trying my best to look nonchalant, still, I wanted to see his face when he took that first bite. As he raised the tainted Oreo to his lips, I was giddy and could hardly contain myself. He was about to jam it into his mouth when he stopped...and looked at me. He must have felt the tension in the air. Maybe he was psychic. "Is there something wrong -- with this cookie?" he asked suspiciously. I clenched my teeth to keep from laughing. "Mmmm...no," I stammered. He took a closer look at it, then pulled it open and sniffed it. "What the hell *is* this?" he said.

I couldn't hold back any longer. I laughed so hard I slumped to the ground. "Man! You were going to let me eat this weren't you! What is this s**t anyway?" I couldn't answer. I held up my hand as if to say, "Please, I can't laugh anymore, you're killing me."

That's how you know when you have a really good friend. He never took another cookie without asking first. He never sought revenge. And he never reminded me of the day I tried to poison him.

The more I listened to this new KXOK, the more I liked it. The guys sounded like they were having so much fun, it was contagious. Each one had a distinctive style and personality and it was fun to tune in and see what new things they had to say. But the guy I liked the best was named Johnny -Johnny Rabbitt. What I liked so much better about him than all the rest was his way of speaking that made me feel he was talking just to me and no one else. Of course, I instinctively knew this couldn't possibly be true. Anyone who owned a radio could hear him, and I was sure there were plenty of other kids out there with radios such as mine. Nevertheless, it was as if this Johnny was speaking directly to me. He became my friend in the night. Soon after that I began to think to myself, "What a wonderful job that must be. Sitting there in a little studio, playing music for people and talking to them, being their unseen friend."

But how in the world does someone get such a job? There must be thousands of people clamoring for such a position. I had no idea where to even begin. I decided the best way to find out was to go right to the source. I called the station. I dialed the phone, more than a little nervously. After all, I was just a kid. I was calling to speak to a DJ named Don Shafer. This is a grown man, I thought – an adult. He'll probably hang up on me. He'll think, who is this dumb kid, asking grown-up questions? But I didn't care about that. I dialed the phone and hoped for the best. The receptionist answered on about the tenth ring. I politely asked to speak to Don. I figured that would be the end right there. She'd probably say, "Mr. Shafer doesn't have time to talk to kids," and hang up. To my surprise, she told me to hold on a moment. Don came on the line and said, "Hi!"

I will always remember that conversation, because he was so nice and helpful, not mean or arrogant at all. He politely listened as I explained that I wanted to know how to become to become a disc jockey? Don laughed and said, "Well, first you have to be a little nuts!" I laughed at this comment and said, "Well, I've got that part down already. What else?" He explained that I would have to take a test to get an F.C.C license and told me that I would have to make

Don Corey

some calls to find out where the testing would be given. I didn't want to keep him on the phone too long and I figured this information would be a good enough start. I thanked him very much for his time and he told me he was "glad to help" and wished me luck. I remember hanging up the phone and thinking to myself, "This is something I really want to do. I don't know where I'm going from here, but I know I'm on the way to somewhere." You know, when you really want something with all your heart, it's just like praying.

FIVE

My grandma's name was Helen Shillito. It sounds Italian but in actuality it's derived from the French. The original spelling was Shilliteau, but it was changed sometime after arrival in America. Helen was a generous woman -- unlike my grandpa Oliver. He was so tight I'm surprised he didn't squeak when he walked.

When I was a young boy, anything my little heart desired Helen would get for me. I never took advantage of this. I did not just ask for things, just to be collecting toys like some of the other kids. I only asked for something to fulfill an "idea" I had. Grandma indulged my sometimes off-the-wall schemes. Perhaps one of the reasons she was so willing to go along with my crazy ideas was, when I was about three years old, I asked her if it was all right to call her by her first name, "Helen," instead of "grandma." She wondered why I would ask this. I replied, "Because you don't look old enough to be a grandma." I did not do this to "schmooze" her by any means. At that age I did not even know what "schmoozing" meant. I was just being truthful. She was, in fact, very young looking. Many times when we were out together at the shopping center, strangers would ask, "Oh, is this your little boy?" Of course she would just beam with delight. At that age I didn't understand it, although I do now. In any case, she said, "Donald, you can call me Helen any day of the week!"

My grandpa, on the other hand, just sort of considered me a necessary evil -- much like having to have to pay taxes. He might not like it, but it comes with the territory. He did have a great sense of humor though. Years later when I started dating, he would kid me by saying, "You'd better be careful bringing your girlfriends around, I'll steal them from you." I'd just laugh it off. But one day I did bring one of my steady girlfriends over to meet him before we left on our date. He joked with her for a while, and then my girl and I left. For the next hour all I heard was, "Your grandpa is so cute. He's so funny. He's so..." I'm thinking, "What am I, chopped liver?" I couldn't believe it. He was right. He was stealing my thunder and he wasn't even there.

So grandpa was funny, but he was not the "go-to guy" for any of my ideas. The only thing that saved me was that in his house, Helen was the boss. If I had another hair- brained scheme that I wanted to carry out, I went straight to the top. And the top was Helen.

Helen and Grandpa

Don Corey

As I said, my grandma Helen was a wonderful woman. Probably the zaniest of all my crazy ideas occurred around 1960 when I was about 11 years old. Our local bowling alley, Marlborough Lanes, had just completely remodeled, adding the New Brunswick A2 Pinsetters. They threw out all kinds of old bowling stuff and I convinced my grandma that it would be "really cool" if we could build a bowling alley in the back yard. I did not, for one minute, figure she would go along with this one. But my grandma had a funny fixation with something she called "ash-pit picking." Apparently, in the "old days" they had something called ash pits where people would throw things away. Grandma used to climb into these things and bring all kinds of treasures home. At least that's how she viewed it. "One man's trash is another man's treasure," she used to tell me. She loved getting things free. If she had to dig around to get it, that was better still.

So when I told her "they're just throwing this perfectly good stuff out," she couldn't resist. She drove me up there in the old Chevy station wagon. With permission from the manager, we loaded up the car with as much stuff as we could. We actually made several trips to get it all. There were bowling balls, pins, and scoring sheet pads. The balls had cracks in them, but that was no big deal. The best were two items of interest. One was the bowling ball return. It looked like a small railroad track and it was the device that would send the ball from the pin area to the foul line. It was 60 feet long broken up into 10-foot sections. Grandma decided we would only take three sections, totaling 30 feet. The reason for this was clear. "I don't want you taking up the whole back yard with this thing."

The second item was my favorite. It was the "sweep arm." It was the item that was originally attached to the pinsetter. It would descend to sweep the lane of any "deadwood" after the first ball was thrown. It had the "Brunswick" logo on it and it was in pristine condition, but that was not to last for long. You see, instead of this piece having to sweep anything away, on my alley it would have the job of stopping the ball before it could careen into the neighbor's yard.

After we dragged this stuff home, it was time to set it all up. My dad graciously supplied some old wall paneling that he had left over from a downstairs project. I enlisted the help of my friend Dave Roberts, who was a year older and just like a big brother. I had no brothers or sisters, so I looked up to Dave who was always there for me, always a great friend. It didn't hurt that he was quite a bit bigger, too. He was tall and could be very imposing when he so chose. One time the two of us were at Steak 'n Shake, sitting in a booth. Some punk kid was giving us a hard time and Dave was sitting down, just listening to this guy spout off. When the guy finished his little speech, Dave stood up -- and up and up. The guy craned his neck to look up at his face. Dave said, "You were saying?" The guy mumbled some sort of apology and quickly exited the building. So when there was a big task, Dave was the big guy who got it done.

Dave and I set about the task of nailing the wood panels onto two-by-fours. We ran the 30-foot bowling ball return to the right side of the lane. The gutters on each side were a little trickier. We didn't really have anything semi-round, but we nailed some scrap lumber together in a "V" shape that would suffice to

Don Corey

hold the ball. It looked pretty raw, but we figured, what the heck...it's only 30 feet long instead of 60, probably won't get that many gutter balls anyway. Meanwhile, the sweep arm didn't always work. Especially when my friend Dave would launch the ball with such force that you thought he was trying to break the sound barrier. The ball would happily fly right past the backdrop, lofting into the air and sailing to the next yard, effectively mowing down several of the neighbors' prized flowers. These neighbors by the way were my mom and dad. Yes, believe it or not, my parents lived right next door to my grandparents.

The bowling alley looked great. I would actually get up at 6 a.m. to polish it with Johnson's wax. I bought some fancy aluminum lettering at the hardware store, the kind used for the address of your home. I picked out nine letters that spelled out "Don's Lanes" and nailed them to a piece of wood, then nailed the sign to a tree in the front yard.

Neighborhood kids would arrive pretty early and want to bowl, but I had to put them off until about noon. The reason for this was the noise. At a real bowling alley, the pins are 60 feet away and there are acoustical ceiling tiles to absorb some of the noise. Not at my alley. You can't imagine the bedlam when that 16-pound ball would hit those pins. Crash! Then it's time to pick the spare. Crash! Set them up again. Crash! There was no electronic pinsetter so we set them by hand. There were 10 circles drawn on the wood surface to show where the pins should go.

The bowling alley was a complete success. All the neighborhood kids loved it. People from blocks away would show up as the word spread like wildfire. Even among the adults. When Mom and Dad would have friends over to play cards, they'd have to come out and see. It's amazing, but years later I can meet someone who says, "Hey, aren't you the guy who had a bowling alley in his back yard?"

Of course, all good things must come to an end. A couple of the adult neighbors complained about the noise. The police department told them as long as we weren't hurting anyone and it wasn't real early in the morning or late at night, there wasn't anything they could do. Not to be deterred, one neighbor somehow got the health department involved and had it declared a "health hazard" because it interfered with people's sleep. They said they slept in the middle of the day. Once the health issue raised its ugly head, the police came back and told us we had to shut it down. The police were very apologetic. I could tell they didn't want to bring this bad news. I guess they figured it was nice to see some kids doing something worthwhile instead of being hoodlums. Nevertheless, "Don's Lanes" closed.

We tore up the old paneling, added more lumber and made a clubhouse. I put the old pins out front for the trash man to take away. I later found out that my friend Steve had taken them out of the trash and was selling them in his front yard. People were buying them up to make lamps. Steve was more of an entrepreneur than I was. The irony of this did not go unnoticed. Another "ash pit picker" outdid me.

Backyard Bowling Alley
Side view

Backyard Bowling Alley
Rear view

Don Corey

I'd like to say my early entrepreneurial ideas all turned out well. But that would not be true. After my bowling alley shut down, I was still felt the need to have some sort of business -- something a few steps higher than a lemonade stand. I considered those types of things too amateurish for my taste. No, I decided on a restaurant. My grandpa had a finished basement. It had a fancy bar with a big mirror and a large assortment of booze. "This would be perfect," I thought to myself. A new sign replaced "Don's Lanes." It read, "Don's Restaurant." I made up several bologna sandwiches, some with mustard, some with catsup, and some plain. I had some small bags of chips and pretzels on hand. And, of course, six ounce Coke in bottles. I even used my mom's typewriter and made an official looking menu. Dave and I would run the place and charge 25 cents a sandwich, a dime for the chips and a dime for the Cokes. We figured, hey, there's no way we can't make a profit. There's no overhead because it's grandma's house. We don't even have to pay for the meat or the bread -- it's all clear profit! What could possibly go wrong? What indeed.

After several days of sitting around waiting for the neighborhood kids to show up and buy our stuff, we said to ourselves, "What's the deal? Nobody's coming in." I piped right up with the answer. "I know! What this place needs is some atmosphere." "What do you mean?" said Dave. "You know ... atmosphere," I said again. I ran to the end of the room and pointed above the fake fireplace at a small shelf that held a candleholder, complete with candle. "All we need to do is light this candle and dim the main lights. That's what they do in those fancy restaurants. The food's not that great, it's just the mood lighting." It sounded logical to Dave and me. We lit the candle and Dave said, "Isn't that candle awfully close to the ceiling? What if the ceiling would catch fire?" I put my hand over the flame and up near where the ceiling was and it felt warm, but not hot. I concluded, "Naw, it's ok."

We dimmed the lights and sat down on the big green sofa to read our comic books -- waiting for that big rush of customers to come rolling in. Several minutes had passed when great grandma Minnie came to the top of the stairs and yelled down, "Are you kids smoking cigarettes down there?" We replied, "No, we're just sitting here reading." She yelled back down. "Well, there's smoke all over the place up here!" I thought to myself, "I really don't see how one little candle could give off that much smoke, but..." I turned to look in the direction of the candle. Seven inches above the candle was a big round hole in the ceiling. The flame that I thought wasn't that hot had gradually burned a hole completely through the ceiling tile. Because smoke rises, it had all gone upstairs, which is why Dave and I were completely unaware that anything was amiss. Now, however, we immediately went into panic mode and yelled, "Call the fire department!"

The call was put in, and being only several blocks from the fire department on South Elm, we figured an engine should arrive quickly. Hopefully they could avert what was turning into a major tragedy. Minutes ticked by. Still no firemen. What could be wrong now? It turned out that my Aunt Lea was walking around in the front yard doing some sort of gardening when the

Don Corey

fire truck came flying down the street. It stopped right in front of the house and they asked, "Is this the house that reported the fire?" Good old Aunt Lea shook her head and said, "No fire here." Now the fire department guys are running up and down trying to figure out which house to go to. Finally Dave and I went to see what was going on. We yelled to the firemen, "Over here, come quick!" Two firemen ran downstairs and quickly removed the one ceiling tile and threw it on the floor, dousing it with a foam fire extinguisher. Thankfully it was a flame-retardant tile, so it hadn't actually caught fire. It was just glowing and smoldering. None of the adjacent tiles were affected and nothing else had caught fire. No collateral damage at all. Except, of course Don's Restaurant closed permanently.

Dad   Mom   Helen   Grandpa

Grand opening of "Don's Restaurant"

Don Corey

It was now time to go to grandma Helen for another big idea. After the restaurant fire fiasco, I figured this had better be a safe idea. I told her I wanted a reel-to-reel tape recorder. She asked what I had in mind. I explained that I wanted to be a disc jockey and I needed to find out how my voice sounded. She simply smiled and said, "We'll go shopping this weekend and see what we can find."

There would be no "ash-pit picking" this time. This would be a brand new machine. Shopping with her was always an adventure, and this trip was no exception. We went to several stores, but in the 60's, tape recorders were hard to find. I guess there wasn't much demand for home recorders. But we did find one by Montgomery Ward.

The brand name was Telectro and it was huge. It was about the size of a medium suitcase and it looked like it might weigh about a ton. It would accommodate up to a seven-inch reel and ran on 110 volts. It even came with a blank reel of "Scotch" recording tape and an empty "take-up" reel.

Grandma wanted the sales clerk to give us a demonstration, but he was either not that interested in making the sale -- or he just didn't know how to work the thing. I thought, "Let me at it. I guarantee I can figure it out." But I kept silent. Grandma looked at me and said, "Is this what you had in mind?" I nodded and said, "Yes." She turned to the clerk. "Write it up-we'll take it with us." I was excited beyond words. This was going to be my best idea yet. I could barely wait to get it home and try it out. I had no idea what calamities were about to unfold.

The maiden voyage with the new recorder is one that I'll never forget. It was like a happening. The whole family was involved. There were Mom and Dad, grandma Helen and Grandpa, Great Grandma Minnie and Aunt Lea. The tape recorder was in the middle of the living room and we all huddled around it in great anticipation. Since I was just "the kid," I just watched as the adults attempted to work this ominous-looking machine. They put the reel of tape on and put it into the record mode. They then passed the microphone around as each member of the family said a few short words. My grandma said a quick line from a nursery rhyme. My Dad just said, "How're ya doin'?" and of course, my grandpa had to tell one of his dumb jokes. Great Grandma Minnie and Aunt Lea didn't have much to say, they were there mostly to watch the festivities. Frankly, I didn't think they were doing it right, but I was just the kid, so I kept my mouth shut and simply observed. If figured I'd have my shot at it soon enough when the novelty wore off.

When everyone finished their little speeches, one of them rewound the tape and hit "playback." We all sat quietly and waited. Nothing. No sound from the speaker at all. After about 30 seconds, they started saying things like, "It's not working." "Maybe the tape is threaded wrong." "We'll probably have to take the damn thing back." and other such mumblings. After several minutes of this annoying discourse, they decided to "give it one more try before it goes back to the store." As for me I sat there dejectedly, thinking, "Please don't take it back, I haven't even tried it yet!"

They rewound the tape and put it back into "record."

Don Corey

But before anyone could say any of their rehearsed lines, sounds began emanating from the speaker. My family had inadvertently recorded themselves when they thought they were playing back! They had the right idea -- just backwards! We listened as the recorder spewed out all the crazy things they were saying when they thought the machine wasn't working. When we heard, "We'll probably have to take the damn thing back," we laughed ourselves silly! They had accidentally pulled an audio version of "Candid Camera" on themselves without knowing it.

We played the tape over and over and laughed at how funny it sounded. At that moment I knew I had an electronic marvel that would provide me with hours of entertainment. I did not, however, anticipate what would occur when my turn came.

Great Grandma Minnie

Don Corey

If I was serious about becoming a radio announcer, I needed to record myself on tape and see what my voice actually sounded like. Sort of like the audio version of looking in a mirror, I reasoned. It seemed logical enough.

I put my new tape recorder into the record position and said a few lines of dialogue in the most professional voice I could muster. Which, of course, wasn't saying much, since I was young and my voice had not matured yet. Nevertheless, I figured, you've got to start somewhere.

I rewound the tape and put it into the playback position. I was horrified at what I heard. This was, without question, the most horrific-sounding person I had ever had the misfortune of hearing. It was incredibly bad. And yet, I knew it *had to* be my voice. Why did it sound so awful? I turned off the recorder. I had to go outside and think about what had just happened.

I was so excited at the prospect of pursuing a radio career. Now all I could think of was, how can I go through life if that's what I really sound like? Why has no one said anything about my voice until now? Is everyone just trying to be kind and not hurt my feelings? Perhaps I could join one of those religious orders where you take a vow of silence.

Many days went by and my grandma would ask, "Are you having fun with your new tape recorder?" I would smile politely and say, "Yes, it's great. I love it." I just couldn't bear to tell her that my hopes and dreams were dashed and in the dirt. I couldn't explain it to her or anyone else because I'm not sure I even understood it myself.

I decided to stop recording for the time being and find something else to occupy my time. My friend Dave and I hit upon a perfect solution. It was big-trash pickup week in Webster Groves and several people had thrown away old TV sets. We used an old wagon to drag several of them home to make a working TV for ourselves.

We knew nothing at all about TV repair, but this was back in the day when television sets used vacuum tubes. So, we reasoned, we would simply pull the tubes out and take them to the nearest Radio Shack or Katz Drug store and test them on their tube tester. The testing of the tubes was free. If we actually had a bad tube, we would find out how much it cost, then save up our money to buy a new one.

We got tired of this very quickly though, when we found out how much the tubes cost. Many of them were way out of our price range. So we decided to do the next best thing. We logically concluded that there just couldn't be that much of a difference between all those tubes. Why not just take some tubes from one set and put them into another set. Eventually we might get lucky and end up with a working TV.

We tried this theory by swapping one tube at a time. We had a long extension cord that allowed us to hide behind Grandpa's bar and peer around the corner as we plugged it in. If nothing dangerous happened, we would inch closer to see if we had sound or a picture. Occasionally fire would shoot out and we'd quickly unplug it, douse it with a small fire extinguisher -- and then put it back out to the curb for trash day.

We did finally end up with a workable solution. We had two TV's that both functioned -- somewhat. One of them had a picture, but no sound. The other had sound, but no picture. We simply butted the two of them next to each other and --- presto --- we now had essentially a working television. We just had to make sure to change the channels so that each set was getting the same program.

Sometimes we'd forget and accidentally switch only one of them. Everything would seem all right for a few minutes, but then we'd notice the person on the screen would be speaking, but the dialogue just didn't match. Depending on what was going on, it could be pretty hilarious. Sometimes we'd even tune in two different channels on purpose to see how funny it could get. On the screen would be some romantic setting with a guy and a girl all snuggled close -- and the audio would be a frantically yammering announcer loudly telling us how to get stains off our teeth.

After I spent several days brooding over my pitiful-sounding voice, I decided to get back to recording again. If this voice is what I'm stuck with, I'll just have to live with it and hope I can eventually improve. It certainly can't get any worse. I answered the phone one day and the person on the other end said, "Is this Mrs. Corey?" Oh, great. Now I sound like a woman! As it happens, my mom actually had a pretty deep voice on the phone and was frequently mistaken for a man.

I went back to the tape recorder and started recording myself again. It was painful to listen to, but as I repeatedly recorded and then played it back, something odd began to happen. I started to get used to the sound of my voice. At first I wasn't sure if the sound was improving or if I was just growing more tolerant. Perhaps it was a little of both. Whatever the reason, it gave me just enough hope to continue and not give up.

Years later I would come to understand this phenomenon. It turns out that when you hear your own voice played back with a high-quality recording device, you hear precisely how everyone else hears you. The reason it sounds so different is that you're used to hearing the sound that projects from your mouth as well as the conduction resonating in your skull. This resonance makes your voice sound more full.

When you hear the playback, all of that good resonance is missing, so it sounds flat and unappealing. If I had known that, I could have spent a lot less time agonizing and more time rehearsing. I still had so far to go and I had barely begun.

Now that I was at least tolerant of my voice, the next step would be how to get myself on the radio. I noticed an item at the Lafayette Radio Electronics store that said, "Broadcast your voice into any radio." Yes, this is the ticket. I would take my pre-recorded voice and broadcast to all my neighbors up and down the block.

I purchased this small device that looked like a rather

large black ice cube. It had five wires sticking straight up from its base. Two of the wires were for the audio, two were for a nine-volt battery, and one was for the antenna. I dutifully hooked it up using the instructions, which came with a warning. It read, "Do not use with more than three feet of antenna wire." I carefully measured out the three feet of wire. After making sure all the connections were right, I put the recorder into the play mode and grabbed my transistor radio. I tuned around on the dial until I located my signal. It was somewhat distorted but, hey, this was my first attempt. At least I had something. I ran outside, excited to see how far the signal would go. It didn't take long to find out. I got to the end of our driveway and the sound all but disappeared. It was a crushing moment.

Undaunted, I ran back inside and decided to tweak it a little. My first thought in this endeavor was, why would the manufacturer say not to use more than three feet of antenna? Surely this must be because more feet would result in a stronger signal. Operating on this assumption, I disconnected the three-foot wire and replaced it with 300 feet of telephone wire. My grandma had brought me this wire during one of her famous scavenger hunts. I hooked up the wire and ran it out my bedroom window. Of course, my parents had no idea this was going on and that's just the way I liked it. They wouldn't understand, I reasoned. I ran the wire to the edge of our back yard and then took the excess and heaved it up into a tall tree. I then took my transistor radio and again checked the signal. To my surprise and utter delight, I found I could now go about three houses down and the signal was still there. This was an exciting moment for me, my very first "radio station" all mine to do with as I pleased. "Oh, wait until the neighbors hear this!" I thought. But then I had another idea. "If the signal increases using 300 feet of antenna, I'll bet it'll go even further -- if I replace the nine volt battery with 110 volts!" Brilliant logic, I thought.

I removed the nine-volt battery, found an old lamp in the basement and removed the cord. After stripping the two wires, I joined them to the transmitter with electrical tape. Now I was ready. This would be a monumental moment in my quest to be on the radio.

I inserted the plug into the outlet. A flash of fire shot out of the cube, followed by a dense cloud of smoke. I quickly unplugged it and waited to see if my parents had noticed that the lights had dimmed. Many was the time, during one of my experiments, my parents would yell out, "Donald, are you messing with something in there?" This time – thankfully -- no one was aware of this debacle except me. The little transmitter now looked like a burnt piece of coal from an active volcano. After it cooled, I gently dropped it into the trash.

SIX

I was in the fourth grade. My favorite DJ was Johnny Rabbitt on KXOK. He was going to appear in person at the Crestwood Plaza. I was very interested in attending this event, but I knew there would be a gigantic crowd. I still really wanted to meet this guy. It was to start early in the morning.

Normally I would have asked my parents to give me a ride to the shopping center, but that wasn't going to work. Number one: They could care less about a personal appearance by a DJ they didn't even know. Number two: This was to occur on a Saturday morning. They always stayed out late for Friday night bowling. They didn't usually get home until 2:00 A.M. and I figured it was not likely they'd drag out of bed that early for my little adventure.

But I did have a plan. They usually didn't get up until about noon on the Saturday after bowling. I could

Don Corey

simply climb out my bedroom window and ride my bike up to Crestwood Plaza. I went to bed early, but I was too excited to sleep. Mom and Dad came rolling in about 2 a.m. I waited until they were sound asleep and then I carefully climbed out my window, grabbed my bike and headed for Crestwood.

It was a beautiful night for a three-o'clock-in-the-morning bike ride. I was sailing along splendidly without a care in the world until a police car flew by. "Uh-Oh!" I thought to myself. "I wonder if he saw me." Yes, what an intelligent question. How could he miss me? The police car pulled onto the shoulder and stopped. As I pedaled up to the side of the patrol car, he rolled down his window.

"Hi there."
"Hello, officer."
"Where are you headed?"
"Uh, I was going to Crestwood Plaza...a DJ from KXOK is going to be there and I wanted to beat the crowd."
"When is that going to happen?"
"About eight or nine."
"And what do you plan to do for the next 5 or 6 hours?"
"I thought I'd just ride around the parking lot."
"I see...are you sure you're not running away from home?"
"Oh, no sir- my life at home is great."
"Well, son, I'm going to have to call your parents."

So much for life at home being great. That was going to end pretty abruptly. He asked for my home number and used his car radio to have the dispatcher patch him in. I stood by the car and helplessly listened to the conversation.

"Hello, is this Duane Corey?"
"Yes, it is. Who is this?"
"This is the Crestwood Police Department. Do you have a son named Donald Corey?"
"Yes, I do. What's this all about? It's three o'clock in the morning!"
"Yes sir, it is. Do you know where your son is right now?"
"Yes, he's in his damn bed asleep!"
"No, he's not. He's standing right here with me on his bicycle. You'll have to come to the station and pick him up."
"Yes sir, I'll be right there."

Needless to say, I did not get to see Johnny Rabbitt that day. I can't remember now if I got a spanking, got grounded or what. I really can't recall. I guess the mind blocks out exceedingly painful memories.

A few weeks later my parents got into an argument. Mom angrily stormed out of the house wearing just her bathrobe. She was driving around aimlessly when she was pulled over by the Crestwood Police. It was about 3 a.m. She told the officer she'd had a fight with her husband. He asked to see her driver's license, but she didn't have it with her. He used his car radio to check with the dispatcher and when he found out her name was Lorraine Corey, he said, "Don't you have a son named Donald?" Yes, it was the very same policeman who met me on my own little 3 o'clock adventure.

One can only imagine the thoughts that ran through

the officer's mind. My dad later commented, "I'll bet the policeman thought, the poor guy's got a lunatic for a son and the wife is nuts too."

I didn't always have my mind on radio. Even though I wasn't good at sports, like any other 12-year-old kid, I still *wanted* to be good at it. So instead of actual baseball games with the other kids, my friends on our block would get together and just practice hitting the ball. Chris, the kid from the end of the block, would pitch. By pitch, I don't mean pitch in the literal sense, like you'd see in a regular game. He would stand maybe five car-lengths away, in the middle of the street, and loft the ball high in the air in our direction. The idea was to have the ball bounce several times. By the time it got to where the batter was standing, it would be at just the right height to swing at it. My friend Steve and I took turns batting and trying to outdo one another. We'd try to see who could hit the ball the farthest.

This little game turned out to be tricky sometimes, because we had to not only drive the ball as far as possible, but also keep it near the center of the street. The reason for this was one of our neighbors. His name was Mr. Landry. He had a really nice lawn and wanted very much to keep it that way. He frowned on any kids running onto his property to retrieve anything. He would yell at us, sometimes confiscating the errant ball. Incidentally, we used tennis balls instead of baseballs for our practices, because they bounced better and if we did hit something with a foul shot there'd be less damage.

One sunny afternoon Steve and I were up to bat with

Chris pitching as several of the neighborhood kids looked on. Steve nailed the ball and it sailed right toward Mr. Landry's house. It crashed into the big awning over his picture window. It sounded like an explosion! You never saw a bunch of kids disappear so fast. Mr. Landry came out on his porch, but there was no one around. We were all hiding in bushes, behind cars, whatever was handy. Game over. Come again another day.

We thought that was bad, but what happened a few weeks later was worse. Once again it was Chris pitching and Steve and I were taking turns hitting the ball. Today however, was slightly different. Instead of taking turns with the same baseball bat, Steve and I each had our own bat. This would soon prove to be a very bad thing.

I had just taken my turn at bat and drove the ball several houses away -- a pretty good hit for me -- and it was Steve's turn to try to beat my distance. Chris retrieved the ball and sent a bouncing pitch our way. The ball came in right where it should have, but Steve foul-tipped it and it fell short of my effort. Naturally, I was quite pleased. It wasn't often that I was able to excel in any sport and this was a nice moment for me. Steve, however, was not pleased. He argued that, since it was a foul tip, it shouldn't count and he should be allowed to take another turn. I insisted that the turn did, in fact, count and that it was my turn again. As the two of us continued bickering, Chris yelled out, "Here it comes!" and let the ball fly. Chris didn't care whose turn it was, he was going to pitch either way. As the ball came bouncing in our direction, Steve and I immediately stopped arguing and squared off, ready to swing. In my mind it was settled, it was my turn. I was concentrating on preparing to belt this one into the next county. I failed to realize that Steve had also squared off and was preparing to do the same thing.

As the ball reached the point of no return, both of us swung at the same time. Steve was directly across from me and as we both swung, he ducked. I didn't. The bat hit me on the right side of my forehead, knocking me to the ground. Strangely, it did not hurt when it happened. I figured I had just been slightly grazed with the bat. Being the eternal joker, I exclaimed, "Call an ambulance. I'm dead." I then reached up with my right hand to touch where the bat had hit me, expecting to feel a bruise. What I felt instead was a huge gash like a miniature version of the Grand Canyon. My hand felt wet. Pulling it down, I saw it was covered in blood. Now I was worried. I had experienced other injuries, but I could tell this one was a lot more serious than any previous mishaps. I scrambled to my feet, saying, "I'll be back later," and headed for mom and dad's house. I went to the back door and as I opened it, I thought to myself, "I probably shouldn't go in, I'm going to get blood everywhere." So I stayed on the back porch and yelled inside, "Mom and Dad come quick, I'm hurt." They took one look and I could read their faces. It was not good.

The next minutes were a blur, but I ended up in the back seat of the car with a cold rag on my forehead as they raced me to St. Joseph's Hospital. It wasn't far away, but the ride seemed to take an awfully long time. My head was throbbing now. I could feel my heartbeat in my head, like a giant headache in a single spot. I vaguely remembered thinking, "I guess this is it. I'm checking out already." I'd never seen that much blood and I was sure there was no way I was going to pull through this one. When we got to the hospital, there was another short period that I can't recall. Then a doctor was stitching me up. He told me it took 35 stitches to close the wound. I had no idea if that was good or bad; I just knew that I was still alive. When I got home, Steve was really glad to see me. I guess he thought he'd killed me. When I got back to school, everyone asked me about the big bandage on my head and wanted to "see the scar." It sounds crazy, but now – I -- felt -- invincible.

Around the time I was 13 years old, my mom and dad would have guests over almost every Saturday night to play cards. This was an exciting time for me, because I knew I would have a "captive audience."

They would always set up a huge table in the living room. The table was normally a square, but when the guests arrived, four hidden angles on hinges just underneath the table swung out and clicked into a lock position. Suddenly the normally large square table became an even larger round table. Out would come the snacks -- pretzels and chips, beer and soda. There were large ashtrays to accommodate the smokers.

Just before the game would get underway, I would sneak in and place a small radio near their card table and then go to my room and "broadcast" a radio show. I made sure to play songs I knew they'd like so they wouldn't tune me out. I'd play "You're Nobody

Don Corey

'Til Somebody Loves You" by Dean Martin, "The Moonlight Gambler" by Frankie Paine, "The Wayward Wind" by Gogie Grant and "Stranger On The Shore" by Mr. Acker Bilk, as well as other old favorites.

The way I obtained this fine music with my limited funds was courtesy of a very nice man named Mr. Roy Gleason, the owner of Webster Records in Webster Groves. When he heard about my little radio station, he kindly gave me a "professional discount" on any 45s I bought. It was a very generous thing to do and I never forgot his kindness. I always told everyone I knew, that if they needed music, Webster Records was the place to go.

When Mom and Dad's guests took a break from their card game, they would stop by my bedroom to see "the station." It was fun to show off the equipment and how it operated. Looking back, when I think of how much equipment and junk was crammed into my small bedroom along with the bed I slept in, it's hard to believe there was room enough for me. It's a good thing I've never been claustrophobic.

This was good training for me, because typically radio station control rooms aren't very big either. When I would listen to radio though, it all seemed "huge." Perhaps it was because in the early days of radio they used a lot of "reverb" which made the room sound bigger. Besides that, the DJs always said things like, "Now we switch you to Studio B for a live report."

Then there were the "jingles." Oh, how I loved the way they sang the station call letters! Another reason I thought the stations must be huge -- I pictured a big group of men and women all standing there, waiting for the cue to sing those call letters. I found out later that they were all on tape. When I first visited a radio station as a kid, I was shocked to see how tiny it was.

But that was the magic of radio. It was all "theatre of the mind." If, in your head you pictured a gigantic room, then it was a gigantic room. That's why I think it's sad when big name movie stars show how they do "voice-overs" for animated cartoons. I liked it better when you believed Daffy Duck really sounded like that. You didn't know it was Mel Blanc; the curtain was never pulled back. I believe it was better that way. When reality is mixed in with fiction, you ruin the illusion.

SEVEN

My 16th birthday was rapidly approaching, so it was time to divert my one-track mind from thoughts of radio, to thoughts of getting my driver's license. Apparently there was a program that would allow me as a teenager to get a reduced price for car insurance. That program was none other than Driver's Education, fondly referred to as Driver's Ed. I was chomping at the bit to drive because, as all guys know, "you can't get the girls without a car." I knew this had to be true. I could not picture coming up to a girl's house for a date and having them hop on the back of my bicycle. Furthermore, I instinctively knew a bicycle date would leave a lot to be desired at the drive-in.

So my parents quickly signed me up. What a class this was! The first few weeks we went over boring stuff like rules of the road, traffic signs and a lot of paperwork. We watched some gruesome movies, showing

Don Corey

horrible accidents to scare us into being responsible drivers. What we wanted was, to get out there and "burn rubber." Before we actually got to go out on the street, we had to use driving simulators. We sat in contraptions that vaguely resembled the front seat of a car -- it had an accelerator and a brake pedal -- and we would watch a movie screen and pretend to drive. This was pretty exciting. If you really concentrated on the screen, it was almost like the real thing. Some sort of monitoring device at the back of the room recorded when we were accelerating versus when we were braking. Occasionally the screen showed someone darting out from between parked cars and that's when we had to hit our brake pedal at just the right instant. It's a good thing these were simulators, because based on some of the scores, there were more than a few simulated children who would never run out from between a car again.

After about a week in the simulators, the time came we had all been waiting for. We would actually drive a real car. You could feel the excitement in the air. Our teacher was a man named Jerry. He was, I would soon learn, a very brave man. We would go out in groups of three. My group had myself and another guy and a girl. Two of us would sit in the back seat, while one of the students would drive. Jerry sat in the passenger seat. He had a special brake pedal on his side so that he could stop the car in case of an emergency.

The first day was pretty lame. We were only allowed to drive around on an empty parking lot. The girl in our group, Karen, was the first to drive. I sat in the back with the other guy as we waited for our turn. The two of us were talking to each other as Karen taxied down the parking lot at a pretty slow clip. I heard Jerry say, "Karen, I want you to bring the car to a nice smooth stop right there in that shaded area of the parking lot." A moment later there was a loud screech. The car lurched forward throwing me and the other guy into the seat in front of us. Karen then said, "Sorry, guys." It had to have been a little disconcerting for her, because from that point on, any time the instructor would say, "come to a smooth stop," she would look in the rearview mirror and see the two of us cringing and waiting for impact.

Eventually Karen got the braking thing down and then it was time to hit the mean streets. It was a day I will never forget. It was Karen's turn behind the wheel and we were cruising down Lockwood in Webster Groves. Thankfully there was very little traffic, so we were feeling pretty safe. We were coming towards a car parked on the right side of the street, when the driver opened his door into the traffic lane. Leaving the door wide open into the oncoming traffic -- namely us -- he then started to fish around for something on the floor of his car. His head was no longer visible to us. At this point we were several car lengths away and Jerry calmly said, "What are you going to do, Karen?" Karen didn't say a word, just kept driving straight ahead, same speed as before. She was doing about three to five miles per hour. Continuing on her present course, she would succeed in tearing this guy's car door completely off. Jerry said, a second time, "What are you going to do Karen?" I could not believe he was saying this so calmly. There was no tension in his voice at all. As for us in the back seat, we watched, wide-eyed, getting ready for what would surely be a spectacular crash. Closer and closer we came, and at the very last second Jerry grabbed the wheel and whipped it to the left. The car veered around the open door, then back into the traffic lane. The man in the parked car suddenly jerked upright as if to say, "What in the hell was that?"

My fellow student and I attempted to start breathing again as we heard Jerry say to Karen, "Pull over in that parking space and stop the car." After she had done this, Jerry calmly said to her, "Now Karen, if I hadn't grabbed the steering wheel when I did, you would have taken that guy's door off. What were you thinking?" Karen just looked at him and said, "I couldn't help it. You were making me nervous!"

EIGHT

I had only been driving for a few weeks. My friend Dave and I liked to "cruise for burgers" in an old Chevrolet station wagon called a Parkwood. My grandpa had given it to me when he upgraded to a new Chevy Impala. It was old, an ugly pale olive drab green with lots of miles on it, but as teenagers we didn't care. It was a "set of wheels" and we were glad to have anything that rolled under its own power. Weekly we would go to the Chuck-A-Burger on Watson Road in Crestwood. The routine was always the same. We parked in a certain spot and turned the headlights on, whereupon a girl would come out to take our order. The girls were always friendly and extremely cute. The food was good, but could have been barely edible. We still would have gone because of the gorgeous carhops.

My order was always the same, too. One burger with catsup and tomato, one small order of fries and one

Don Corey

Coke. I never departed from this order, it was always that, plus whatever Dave was in the mood to eat. They would bring out the food, I would hand it all to Dave and he'd open the glove compartment pull-down door and stack the food on it. He would have to hand the food to me, because the car dome light didn't work, and the place we always parked wasn't very well lit. "All the better to see the girls," we figured. One eventful night we pulled into the parking lot in our usual space. I turned on the headlights and the girl came out and took our order. For some reason, this time I must've felt a little extra hungry because I departed from my "usual" and got two burgers, one fry and one Coke. Later, when she brought out our order, I relayed it from the window to Dave and he placed it on the glove compartment door just like always. He handed me the burger, fries and Coke and we proceeded to "scarf it down" while keeping a running commentary on whatever craziness was going on at the time. I finished the burger and fries, but I completely forgot I had another burger. Dave forgot too. When I asked him to hand me the trash to put back on the tray, he handed it to me and slammed the glove box shut. Neither of us knew that the second burger had flipped into the glove compartment. We paid our bill and drove away.

One week later we were back at our usual spot. Lights on. Girl takes order. Girl brings order. Dave opens the glove box door as I hand him the food. It's still dark in our normal parking spot. I take a sip of my Coke and tell Dave, "Hey man, hand me my burger." Dave hands it to me and I begin to open the wrapping paper and I think to myself, "This doesn't feel very hot." I open the wrapper and feel the bun.

66

"This bun feels stale," I said out loud. Then I pull back the top half of the bun and lean toward the window where the light is a little better. "Oh, my God, look at this, it's got mold on it!" I showed it to Dave and we were both appalled! I immediately turned on the headlights and the girl came back out to see if we needed anything else. "Look at this!" I said as I shoved the burger toward the open window. Her eyes got real wide and she said, "Oh my gosh! I don't know how that could have happened!" Of course I was righteously irate. Before I could say anything more, she said, "I'll go back in and get you another burger." As indignantly as possible I said, "Yes, I think that would be a *very good idea!*" She ran off and Dave and I could see people through the big glass window, running here and there, pointing to one another and shouting. The two of us began to wonder how in the world something like this could happen. A big sign in the window said "Under New Management" and we both wondered aloud, if this is how the new management operates, maybe we'd better start eating somewhere else -- beautiful girls notwithstanding.

The girl quickly returned with a new piping hot burger, still apologizing profusely for the mix-up. By now I had cooled off a little and accepted her apology. She left and Dave and I finished our meal. I asked Dave to hand me the trash and started putting it on the tray outside my window. When he got to the last napkin, he said, "What's with this other burger?" I said, "What other burger?" Dave said, "There's another burger right here." I said, "That can't be; I only ordered one burger and I just ate it. Did you order two?" Dave said, "No way. I only ordered one." All of a sudden we both looked at each other and remembered the previous week. I said, "I ordered two burgers, but I only ate one. That other one must have ended up in the glove compartment and that's the one you handed me. That old burger was here in the car the whole time! What are we going to do?" We were really freaked out now! We decided we'd better get out of there.

We turned on the headlights to summon the girl back to pay the bill. I gave her a big tip, but she was still apologizing and I was saying, "Oh, don't worry about it, these things can happen." We paid the bill, got out of there and never went back again. I can still remember that horrible feeling of guilt. I would never purposely take advantage of someone. I felt like a crook. I never wanted to feel like that again.

I sometimes found myself in sticky situations even when trying to do the right thing. I had just parked my car at the Yorkshire Shopping Center in Webster Groves. Out of the car and heading for a store, I saw a shopping cart on the sidewalk. A stiff breeze was blowing which turned the cart slightly; it started down the hill toward Watson Road. It was a pretty steep incline and I thought, "This should be interesting. When the cart reaches the bottom of the hill it will be going at a pretty fast clip. Might be funny to see what happens."

Where was the cart going? It was headed toward a parked car. This car was no clunker. It was a sharp looking 1964 Mustang. I thought about how upset I would be if an out-of-control cart rammed *my* car. I instinctively took off running after the cart with the intent of stopping the collision. When I entered this chase, I wasn't far away from it, so I didn't see any problem being a "good Samaritan." But the cart picked up speed as it raced down the hill. Although I was right behind it and running fast, it was still an inch away from my grasp.

My mind sped up too as I thought, "I really have to catch this thing now. Before, it was just a case of doing a 'good deed.' Now that I'm in it, if the guy who owns this car sees me, he's never going to believe it's not my cart!"

Usually in a grocery store, you get the cart with the wobbly wheel -- not this one. This cart was flying as straight as an arrow as if to dare, "Try and catch me, son."

With my last burst of energy I reached forward and grabbed hold of the bar. But it was sailing so fast it wouldn't stop. It was really close to the car now. I was almost out of time. I thought, "If I can't stop it, maybe I can just steer it to the right."

I moved my hand all the way to the right side of the bar and yanked hard. The cart veered to the right, tipped over and crashed to the ground. It skidded along the pavement with me right behind it, trying hard not to trip over it. It came to rest about six inches to the right of the car and a foot in front of it. I could barely believe it! I was out of breath, but relieved. Had it not been stopped, it would have demolished that fine automobile.

I hardly had time to collect myself when I heard

Don Corey

cheering and applause coming from the sidewalk. I turned to look and saw a handful of spectators. They had witnessed the entire event. They must have seen me running and wanted to see if I would be able to stop the speeding missile. They smiled and waved appreciatively. I felt drained, but managed a smile and a feeble wave. As the crowd dispersed, I thought, "I had no idea this 'good deed' stuff could be so exhausting."

NINE

When I was 16 years old my dad was diagnosed with diabetes, so he had to change his diet drastically. This affected the family in a number of ways, but one of those led to a funny happenstance. When he went on his strict diet, he shed a lot of pounds. I mean a lot. He dropped several inches in his waist size, which caused him to go out and buy all new clothes. Including new underwear. Dad hated to see things go to waste, so instead of throwing away his old ones, he just put them all in a big cardboard box and put them into the trunk of his car.

Keep in mind that my mom was a very good-looking woman. She had that high-class look just like a movie star. It was fun for me when I was a young kid. Anytime the parents were summoned to the school for some kind of play, everyone would whisper and say, "Who is that blond?" and I'd say, "That's my mom!" They'd looked at me incredulously and said, "No way!" But it was true.

That became the set-up for what would become one of our favorite family stories. Mom's car failed to start one day, so she asked dad to ride with my grandma Helen downtown so Mom could borrow his car. This was arranged and she drove his car to work. So far so good, but she had to pick up groceries on the way home. With a big party planned over the weekend and several couples coming to play cards, she wanted to be sure there was plenty of food to eat. So right after work she went to the local supermarket.

She got a full cartload of groceries, including several cartons of soda that meant carrying home glass bottles. All in all, a pretty heavy load. When she finished paying, the cashier asked if she would like to have "help out to your car." Normally mom would not have done so, but she figured there was a lot of heavy stuff this time, so why not.

A young man piloted the cart out to the parking lot as mom directed him to the correct car. She turned the key in the trunk lock. The moment it flew open, there was probably 70 pairs of different color boxer shorts strewn everywhere. The young man took one look at this and his eyes grew wide. My mom quickly recovered, saying "O.K., I think I can handle it from here."

The kid hurried back to the store as mom quickly tried to get everything into the trunk and leave. She looked back and saw him and several of his coworkers looking out the window in her direction. One can only imagine the thoughts that were running through their heads.

Mom came home and said to Dad, "Well, thank you very much for the use of your car!" When she told us what had happened, Dad and I flew into fits of laughter. "Oh sure, it's all very funny for you," she said. She was quite right. It *was* all very funny for us.

My Mom

Well, it was back to the drawing board for my bedroom radio station. And back to Lafayette. This time I had to save my allowance for several weeks. I had my eye on a new transmitter. This one was much nicer with a powerful look to it. Shaped like a small toaster, it was darkish blue with a tiny slotted screw in the front that was used to tune it to the desired frequency. It came with the same dire warning about antenna length, which, of course, I would choose to ignore. Can't fool me on that one. But there would be no voltage mishaps on this go-round. This one already had a 110-volt plug. It even had an audio input, not like the bare wires I had to contend with on the previous model. I just did not see how this could go wrong.

I plugged in my tape machine with the pre-recorded tape of my practice announcing and hooked up my 300-foot antennae. I placed the machine into the play position and headed off down the street. Past Grandma's house, past the Buchmanns--- I even got as far as the Roberts house and the signal was still coming in strong! I now had my very own radio station. Sure, it didn't go far, but by God it was a start.

My next priority was how to program my station. At this point there was one microphone, one tape deck and one transmitter. But this was not going to stop me. My dad had an old Girard turntable abandoned in the basement somewhere when he got the new "Stereo" in the living room. By my rules, any piece of equipment collecting dust in the basement for more than two weeks was subject to being taken over by me in the name of science. I did not have a mixer, but I got around that obstacle by first recording a record, then announcing the name of the song. I would then repeat until I had a 30-minute program. It was choppy, but it was the best I could do with limited equipment -- also limited resources. Every bit of my allowance was being channeled into this project. I did not dare ask Grandma for anything else. She had already been more than generous.

I would put on my 30-minute "program" and run down to the neighbors' houses and tell them where on the dial they could tune to hear my "show." The neighbors acted like it was "cute" when I told them, but I'm sure as soon as I left they'd turn off the radio and say, "The kid's got a screw loose." I didn't care. I was on my way.

Later I would add a mixer from Radio Shack and two cassette decks, making the programs much smoother and more professional sounding. I was finally making progress.

In 1967 my good friend Jon Liston told me his father worked at a place in Sunset Hills called E.J. Korvette. It was a large department store that sold men's and women's apparel, house wares and they even had a pet shop with birds and dogs. He said there was a job there I might find interesting. It was the "Store Announcer." *Might* be interested? I ran up there the very same day, applied for the position and got it.

Well, this was truly exciting. "It may not be radio," I thought to myself, "but it's a job, and it's announcing and that's as close as I'm going to get right now." Although I was pleased at the prospect, it wasn't exactly the most glamorous position. Not only was I the announcer, I was also in charge of the lost and found department. Yes, shoppers would ask Carol, the telephone operator, if she had found an umbrella (we got tons of those) or perhaps some sunglasses (had a barrel full of those.) She'd say, "Yes, go see Don in the announcer's room." People would stop in while I was making my announcements and then we'd paw around through the junk box.

My announcements went something like this: "Shoppers, now in our Men's Furnishings Department, men's suits which are regularly $34.95 are now just $29.95! That's in the Men's Furnishings Department, on the main level." I would usually make a new announcement every 15 minutes or so. I once mentioned to Jim, the men's department manager, that whenever there was a "15-minute special" in house wares, it seemed to me the housewives would barrel over there and buy things they didn't even need just because it was a "special." Jim did not agree with this assessment, so I told him, "Well, just listen carefully to my next 15 minute special and watch what happens." Having set this up, my next announcement went like this: "Shoppers, for our next 15-minute special, our house wares department has frying pans, regularly $7.99, for just $9.99. That's right, shoppers, for the next 15 minutes those frying pans, regularly $7.99, are just $9.99! Hurry now to our house wares department on the main level." When I called Jim on the inter-store phone, he said, "You were right, there was a mob of people who ran over and bought them up like we were giving them away!" I said, "You see, all they hear is the word 'special' and they go berserk." No one noticed the price went up instead of down. I didn't make a habit of this; doing it one time made the point.

Don Corey

I was also in charge of making announcements if someone got lost. An employee from one of the departments would call and say, "Have so-and so meet Mr. Smith at the Jewelry Counter," or some such thing. My coworkers tended to be practical jokers, so I always had to be careful with what I said over the speaker system. Sometimes they would try to get me to say something dirty by making up a fictitious name, but I was always cautious with these announcements. I would say it to myself before I turned on the microphone, just to be sure. They did get me once though. Someone called and said, "We need you to page a man to meet his son at the bottom of the escalator." So I asked, "What's his name?" They said, "It's Mr. Stares. His first name is Don." So I said, "You got it." I said the name to myself, "Don Stares." There's nothing obscene about that. So I keyed the microphone and said, "Don Stares to the bottom of the escalator." I no sooner had the words out of my mouth than I heard the raucous laughter coming from the sales floor and I knew I'd been had!

My year at E.J. Korvette was a really enjoyable experience. I learned to be professional with my announcing under odd circumstances. My jokester coworkers, when I was doing an announcement, would do things to try to mess me up. Sometimes they would make faces at me, another time one of them poured a glass of water down my back. Probably the worst was the night they lit my script on fire. I quickly scanned the page and dropped the paper, finishing the sentence from memory.

One night two young guys came around the corner into the announce booth and asked if I was the announcer. I figured they must be here to paw through the lost-and-found department, but I was wrong. These two guys wanted to know how I got this announcing job because they wanted to become DJs. Imagine my surprise when they told me they had their own "homemade" radio stations. I was immediately interested. They told me where they lived and invited me to come over. I had no idea that this was going to make a marked turn in my own quest to be a real radio announcer.

The two fellows I met at E.J. Korvette were named Tom and Mark. They both lived in Chesterfield and were most definitely "radio wannabes." My first visit was to Tom's radio station. It was in his parent's basement and was much more elaborate than mine. Even though it was makeshift, he actually had two turntables and a decent mixer. Still, you could tell he had put it together himself. Then we went over to Mark's house just a few miles away. His setup was incredible. It was obvious he had some adult supervision or help building it. There a professional looking main studio, complete with two turntables and a boom microphone, there was another control room with a glass window between them. He even had an intercom so the engineer and the DJ could communicate between songs. Very impressed with both their studios, at the same time I was saddened that mine was so crude in comparison. Nevertheless, I've always said you have to do the best with what you have and be grateful. The big question now was, with studios looking great, how far does your signal go? In this regard all three of us were on common ground. Like me, they had equipment purchased at Radio Shack and the signal only went a few houses,

Don Corey

even with modifications. However, they had a plan that would entail a much bigger reach.

They had not done it themselves, but they knew someone who had. They told me, in hushed tones, that they "knew a guy" who made a transmitter that would not only reach a couple of houses, but several miles! Apparently this fellow had modified a short wave radio in such a way that it would broadcast on the AM band. They were afraid to do this themselves, because it was highly illegal. But they offered to put me in touch with him.

With a feeling that we were sleuths, they gave me his number. I met with him and we worked out a deal. I traded him some of my electronic equipment and he gave me the transmitter. He warned me it would be in my best interest to only stay "on the air" a few hours a day to reduce the likelihood of getting into trouble with the Federal Communications Commission. We made the switch and I hooked my new device into my makeshift studio and prepared to give it the old "field test." Needless to say, my parents had no idea this was about to occur. As far as they knew, this was still the old radio station I had always fooled around with in my room. Unable to tell one transmitter from another, they might have thought it was a toaster. They were just glad I had a hobby and wasn't running around "getting into trouble."

In any case, the moment had arrived. I put one of my pre-recorded tapes on, turned on the new transmitter and ran outside. I hopped into my car and tuned to the correct frequency. It was at about 690 on the dial, just up a ways from KXOK at 630. The signal sounded strong -- not weak like those other devices from Lafayette and Radio Shack. I backed out of the driveway and headed down the street. I passed the first three houses where my signal had previously faded out. It still sounded great. I went several miles down Watson Road (Highway 66) and it still came in as strong as the other stations. I was thrilled beyond words! My little radio station -- I could barely believe it! I jumped onto Highway 244. I was all the way to the Manchester exit and my signal still came in strong! Now, instead of being thrilled, I was beginning to get scared. Yes, I had wanted my signal to get out further, but this was getting a little crazy! The further it goes out, the more people will hear it, and the more I am likely to get caught! I exited at Manchester and hurried home to turn off my equipment. It would be like that for the next few months -- excited to be "on the air" but afraid of seeing an FCC truck pulling up outside the house.

I went so far as to bury an underground cable over to my grandma's house next door. The studio was at my house, the transmitter next door at her house. I figured if the FCC truck triangulated the signal, it would be at the wrong house, giving me a few precious moments to shut everything down. It was fun, but it was nerve-racking.

When nightmares recurred frequently, I knew I would have to shut it down. The dream was always the same. I would be miles from the house, listening to my own little station and a big truck would pass me at a pretty fast clip. On the top of the truck would be a large letter "F." A few moments later another truck would fly by on my left with a large letter "C" on top.

Don Corey

It wasn't until yet another truck went by, with another "C" on the top that I suddenly realized this must be the FCC heading to my house! Increasing speed, I was driving way over the speed limit now, but I could not catch up to them as they were going too fast! Then I suddenly wake up, my heart pounding in my chest. That's it. The bootleg station was fun, but it has got to go.

Like an addict that must have "just one more" fix, my intention of pulling my illegal bootleg station off the air permanently was easier said than done. I was now in my senior year of high school and still putting the station on the air about once a week. I used my pre-recorded tapes and hooked up the entire operation to an appliance timer. It was rigged to come on about 15 minutes before the end of the school day, so I could listen to my show on my car radio as I drove home from school. I reasoned that it was just an hour or so and, after all, the nightmares had pretty much stopped. One day while driving home, I saw a young guy about my age hitchhiking. I picked him up and as we were traveling along I thought it might be fun to impress him a little. I said to him. "You hear the song playing on the radio? That's my radio station." He smiled and said, "Uh-huh." But I could tell he didn't believe me. So I said, "Really. Right after this song the DJ, who is actually me, will say, 'that was the Beach Boys and now here's the Supremes.'" Again he nodded, but I could still tell he didn't believe me. He was just humoring me. Then the song ended and I turned the radio up just slightly as the DJ said, "That was the Beach Boys and now here's the Supremes." The guy turned and looked at me as if I were from another planet and said, "Uh, this is where I get off."

Are You Talking To Me?

He continued staring wildly as I drove away.

About a week later something happened that finally made me more serious about pulling the plug. My friend Mark, who had given me the phone number to get the transmitter, wanted very much to go "on the air" at my station. I was a bit reluctant at first, since I'd already been on the air an hour a day and hadn't been caught. I really hated to stretch my luck. Still, he was a nice guy and really wanted to be in radio. I knew that feeling so well. Besides, I reasoned, this would be a great opportunity to hear my station "live" without having to listen to my own pre-recorded tapes. So I relented. He came over one weekend while my parents were away. I showed him the setup. I let him play a few songs with announcements in between until I was satisfied that he had it down. Then I headed to my car for another "field trip." I drove the same route as I did the first time -- Highway 66 to 244 North. The signal was strong and sounded great. Mark was doing a fine job, no dead air, no mistakes. I felt on top of the world. Then the unthinkable happened.

Mark had just finished playing a song and he said, "That was the Beach Boys with 'Sloop John B.' Say, if you want to hear a request, call now at 961..." Oh my God! He was giving out my home phone number on the radio! I almost ran off the road! I quickly exited the highway and stopped at the first gas station I could find that had a pay phone. I threw the car in park and jumped out with the engine still running. I jammed coins into the pay phone and called the house. It rang once and Mark answered in a professional sounding voice as I screamed into the

Don Corey

receiver, "Are you out of your mind? Shut off the transmitter!" He said, "Right in the middle of the song?" I said, "Yes, right in the middle of the song! We're a bootleg station! You might as well write the FCC and give them my address!" I ran back to my car and right in the middle of the song the station went off the air. That was officially the last broadcast.

In disguise at the helm
of my homemade radio station
1968

Don Corey

My long loyalty to KXOK and the Johnny Rabbitt show was about to change. My grandpa had an ancient-looking radio in the basement that he never listened to anymore. I begged, pleaded and aggravated him until he gave it to me. The radio, a wooden monstrosity with a dark mahogany finish, had a long complicated-looking frequency display. The reason for this was that it received not only AM (Amplitude Modulation) but also FM (Frequency Modulation) and two different bands of SW (Short Wave.)

This was a whole new experience. I now had a multitude of stations to choose from, each one having a diverse possibility of sounds. I spent hours tuning all across the dial to see what I could find. I didn't care much for either of the shortwave channel selections. Although it pulled in signals from far away, I found them interesting, but not very entertaining. I had already heard most everything AM had to offer, so my last stop was FM.

Scanning across the dial, most of it I would describe as "adult music." It was violins...orchestra...not very peppy. This pretty much dominated the whole FM dial. Suddenly I ran across something that caught my attention. In the midst of all this "soothing" music, out jumped a different sound. I immediately recognized the vocalist as Mick Jagger of the Rolling Stones. But this was a song I'd never heard before. KXOK had always played "Satisfaction" and "Jumping Jack Flash," but this song was totally unique. It was a strange, compelling song with contemplative lyrics, quite unlike anything the AM stations played. I found out later it was called "Sympathy For The Devil." Intrigued, I just had to stay tuned until I figured out what this station was I had stumbled upon. Finally the last of the song faded out and I heard, "That was the Rolling Stones...and I'm Steve Rosen...on K-SHE Ninety Five...under St. Louis."

What the heck did that mean? Is the station really under ground? What about the tower? Is it underground? How would that work? How is it they're playing songs I've never heard before by artists I have heard before? And another thing -- this Steve Rosen didn't sound like a "typical" DJ. I'm not sure what that meant, but he sounded -- different. This much I did know. I never went back to KXOK again. This KSHE 95 would be my new home, my new favorite -- my new obsession.

I had a new idea. I recorded a simulated radio show as an audition tape using my home studio. I decided to take this tape and a resume to KSHE. I looked up the address in the phone book. It was 9434 Watson Road in Crestwood.

I tried to find the station but it wasn't as easy as I thought it would be. I could see the tower. At 400 feet tall, it was hard to miss. But I couldn't see how to get to the station itself. The building was back from the highway, not visible from the street. I finally left my car at the Park Crestwood Apartments and walked up a grassy knoll to get there.

I discovered then why I hadn't been able to find the driveway. From the highway you had to pull in as though you were going to the 66 Park In drive in theatre but then you had to veer to the left instead of the right, which was the KSHE driveway.

Don Corey

I turned in my tape and resume to the receptionist. "Some resume," I thought to myself. All that was on it was my one announcing job as the E. J. Korvette store announcer. I didn't bother to mention that I was in charge of the lost and found. I left and went home... to wait for the phone call I feared would never come.

TEN

It was January of 1968. My dream of getting a job in radio was going to have to wait, because it was time to decide which branch of the service I would join. I was interested in the Air Force but disqualified because I was colorblind. But I figured the Army would take anyone with a pulse. My mom talked to some friends in high places and said she could get me into the Army Reserves. First, I had to take a physical exam. I was a little worried about this so I asked my friend Dave, who went through it when he joined the Air Force. His advice: "Just do exactly what they tell you -- nothing more, nothing less -- and you'll be all right."

Fair enough. I headed to the Mart Building downtown. About 40 other guys and I had to strip down to our underwear. We then lined up single file and followed a yellow line on the floor. After several feet, we came to an intersecting line at which we would stop and get instructions. I remembered Dave's advice, so was being careful to do exactly what I was told. At the first station the sergeant said, "Stick out your arm!" I stuck out my arm. He attached a blood pressure cuff and wrote some numbers on a sheet of paper. He then barked. "Move to the next station!" The next man yelled, "Stick out your arm!" Again I stuck out my arm. He stuck me with a needle and then yelled, "Move to the next line!" I moved to the next line. A man handed me a small plastic cup. "Pee in this cup," he ordered. I began to pee in the cup when he yelled, "In the bathroom, stupid!" That was embarrassing. The guys behind me were laughing like idiots. I was simply doing exactly what I was told -- no more, no less. I'd never been in this building before, so how was I to know they even had a bathroom? But it wasn't over yet. After several more stations I arrived at the end. The man behind the counter looked at my paper and turned to his fellow employee and said, "This guy only weighs 113 pounds. Can he go to basic?" After thinking for just a second, he said, "Yeah." I wanted to say, "Hey, let's think about this," but it was too late. He took a big rubber stamp and -- boom! -- Stamped my paper with the word "Accepted."

By February of 1968, I was officially an Army Reservist. I thought I'd be taking basic at Fort Leonard Wood, but my orders sent me to Fort Polk. Louisiana! What a shocker this was. I asked my friend Dave, who had previously given such good advice, what he thought my next move should be. He said, "When you get there, try to blend in. The longer you can go without them knowing your name, the better you'll be." I made a note of this and hoped this advice would serve me better than the first.

I was pretty nervous about this whole trip and not just because I was headed off to boot camp. The other thing that made me a bit jittery was that I'd never flown before. I was booked on Delta Airlines leaving St. Louis at 9:10 A.M. The first flight took me to Memphis and from there I took Delta again to Jackson. So far, everything was fine. On the final leg of the flight things got a little dicey. The last plane was not a big commercial airliner, but a small twin prop job. It didn't look very safe. I climbed aboard, sat back and tried to relax. Take off was a little nerve-racking but soon we were flying along and I convinced myself that everything was going to be fine. At about 12:14 P.M. we were making our final approach to Fort Polk. I was in the window seat watching as the plane began to descend. What I did not know was that the landing strip was cut out of the middle of a forest. The plane would have to come in steep, get the wheels down and the brakes on before the runway runs out. All I knew was what I saw out that window, and the tops of trees were getting closer each second. Any closer, I might have been able to see birds feeding their babies. I seriously thought we were going to crash! I looked around to see if anyone was panicking, but no one else was paying any attention. They were all reading magazines and seemed blissfully unaware that we were going to die.

I made sure my seat belt was firmly fastened and braced myself for the impact I imagined was only seconds away. Suddenly there was a screech of tires and we were on the ground. As we taxied to a stop, while the other guys were getting their belongings, I was as limp as an old washrag. Happy to be alive, but already exhausted -- and the ordeal of basic hadn't even begun. As I walked out the door, the stewardess said, "I hope you enjoyed your flight." I said nothing but thought, "Oh yeah, I can't wait to do that again."

Upon arrival at Fort Polk, we were taken to something called the reception center, which sounds a lot more pleasant than it actually was. The people working there were not drill sergeants but Department of the Army civilians; civilians may have been their job title, but they weren't very civil. Already we could tell there was trouble brewing.

We were taken to a room for our Army haircut. I didn't expect this to be much of a surprise. I'd seen Gomer Pyle reruns enough to know it was a simple buzz cut. But a funny thing happened to the guy sitting in the chair to my left. He had some of those "pork chop" sideburns like Elvis used to have. I heard the barber say to him, "You want to keep your sideburns?" The guy perked right up and said, "Sure!" So the barber took his clipper and lobbed them right off. "Here," he said, as he handed them to him.

Later we went to the mess hall for our first Army meal. Each of us grabbed a tray and walked along a buffet line with army cooks on the other side handing out the food. I was the third man back. I heard the guy ahead of me make an unusual request. He said to the huge cook, "Would you try to not let the mashed potatoes touch the meat?" He then held his tray toward the cook. I did not know much about the Army at this point, but I instinctively knew this would not end well. I figured this was roughly the equivalent of asking a drill sergeant to "fluff my pillow for me." I stood back as the cook picked up a huge spoon -- I'd never seen one that big -- and heaved a gigantic mound of potatoes in the general direction of the tray. An insignificant amount actually hit the plate of food. Most of it went all over the guy in front of me, as well as the guy in front of him. "Move out!" the cook yelled angrily. When it was my turn, he glared at me as if to say, "You got any special requests?" I gingerly held out my tray and quietly took whatever came my way.

It was apparent that Fort Polk was not going to be a picnic. I immediately brought my mind back to that fine piece of advice my friend Dave had given me about blending in: The longer you go without them knowing your name, the better. I tried my best to heed this advice, but when you're a skinny 113-pound beanpole of a human being, it's really hard not to stand out.

I hadn't been there long when I overheard a mean-looking drill sergeant say to another sergeant, "You see Corey over there? I'll bet you ten dollars he'll be the first person to fall out on the five-mile force march." I then heard the other guy say, "You're on." The second guy then came up to me and got real close to my face and hissed, "I've got ten dollars riding on your skinny ass. If you fall out on the force march I'll kick you all the way there." Well, so much for not getting noticed. I had no idea what a force march was, but I'd find out soon enough.

I began to regret the easy-go-lucky lifestyle I had

Don Corey

lived up until now. As a kid I always tried to take the easy way out. If someone would give me $10 to mow a lawn I'd find somebody who'd do it for five and I'd keep the change. Now I was at basic and nobody was going to do my work for me but me. We would get up at the crack of dawn and do something the drill sergeants called "the dirty dozen." It was 12 different exercises with 12 repetitions of each. This was brutal enough, but was just a warm-up to the force march. The force march consisted of a five-mile journey in which we carried a full backpack and an M14 rifle. We had to run a mile, walk a mile, and run another mile without stopping for a break, until we got to the rifle range -- a total of five miles. I'm not sure in my youth I had ever walked a mile, much less run one.

The big day came and, of course, it was the hottest day I ever felt. We started out marching first, then running, walking, and running. It felt like it would never end. At about what I thought was the halfway mark I already felt I couldn't go on. But I knew I had to. The drill sergeant had threatened me and I was quite sure he would make good his intention. I kept marching and running until my legs felt like lead. I was sweating profusely now and I was so thirsty I felt as if I had just swallowed a handful of dry sand. At one point we passed a mud puddle and I wanted to fall down and drink it. Several guys had fallen to the ground. Some of them were overweight but a couple of them were muscular and strong. I couldn't believe they had dropped out and I was still going. Drill sergeants swarmed over them like angry bees and began yelling curse words at them. A few were weeping; some of them were throwing up. I paid no attention. I just kept moving my legs, trying to think of a favorite song in my head that would keep me from feeling the pain.

Finally the rifle range came into view over the crest of a hill. I could barely believe it. I had actually made it to the very end. I was exhausted, yet elated! Here I was, the proverbial "113-pound weakling" who managed to go where stronger men could not tread. I was quite pleased with myself but at that moment a drill sergeant came up to me and said, "I lost ten dollars on account of your skinny-ass. I'm going to be watching you."

When we got to the rifle range I could tell the fun had just begun. I had never fired a weapon before and I was more than a little intimidated by it. I climbed down into the concrete bunker and tried to remember everything the drill sergeants had taught us about correct firing procedures.

When the buzzer sounded, I took aim and tried my best to hit the center of the target. The sound of the rifle blast so close to my right ear was jarring, but it was to be no match for what came next.

After the "all clear" command went out, we all gathered our targets for the drill sergeants to inspect. The idea was to find the holes in each target where the bullet had passed through. This was called your "shot group." If the holes were to the right of where they should be, then you would calibrate your rifle to make the next group hit further left. These controls were called "windage and elevation." Before the sergeant arrived at my station I looked at my target.

Don Corey

My "shot group" was not a group at all. The holes were all over the place. I wondered why this was so. I did not have to wonder long. The drill sergeant took one look at my target and said, "Your shots are all over the place! You're scared of that weapon. You're jerking the trigger. I am going to help you."

All right. He's going to help me. This is great. He told me to aim at the target and ever so slowly, pull the trigger -- gently. I squeezed the trigger and -- bang! Immediately following the recoil of the rifle, the drill sergeant hit me up side my helmet with a wooden paddle. Now my ears were really ringing. "You jerked the weapon," he said. "Try it again." I aimed carefully and tried to squeeze the trigger gently. Bang! Bong! He slammed the wooden paddle against my helmet again, harder this time. "You jerked the weapon again." I was getting a headache now and my senses were reeling. I squeezed the trigger once more and this time the gunshot was not followed by a paddle to my head. "That's the way -- you didn't jerk the weapon that time. I told you I'd help you." Yes, thank you, drill sergeant, I thought to myself. I always secretly wanted a concussion.

After several sessions of practice rounds at the rifle range the big day came when we were to "qualify." This was one of our final tests to see who was the best shot. As we marched to the range I was wearing my glasses because I was very nearsighted and could not see targets so far away. One of my fellow soldiers stepped on the back of my boot, which caused me to trip. My glasses fell to the ground and were broken beyond repair. I immediately began to panic because I knew there was no way I could make a decent showing without those glasses. As soon as we stopped at the edge of the range, I ran up to the senior drill sergeant to explain what had happened.

"Drill sergeant, Private Corey reporting."
"What do you want, Corey?"
"My glasses got broken, Drill Sergeant."
"That's not my problem."
"But Drill Sergeant, I won't be able to..."
"Get out of here!"

You cannot argue with a drill sergeant. His word is law. I went back to the front of the firing line. I knew what would happen, but there was nothing I could do.

The command came, "Ready on the firing line," followed by "Firing line ready. Commence firing!" I heard the buzzer go off, but everything was a complete blur. I fired my rifle in the general direction of where I knew the targets to be and tried my best. Maybe it won't be so bad, I hoped. Within minutes came the command, "Cease firing." The targets were labeled and collected and we marched back to camp. At that point, nothing was said about our scores so I thought maybe I'd gotten lucky.

Back at the barracks we all stood in formation at attention. Senior Drill Sergeant Chappell stood on the high-rise wooden platform in front of us and barked, "At ease." He then proceeded to give the results of the day's today's qualifications.

"Men, we had a real good showing at the range today. We had 69 marksmen, 23 sharpshooters and seven experts! Everyone did a fantastic job... except for one person..." Oh no, I thought to myself. "PRIVATE COREY, GET UP HERE!"

I ran up to the platform, saluted and said, "Private Corey reporting." The drill sergeant turned me around to face the company and shouted, "Private Corey here only hit three targets out of fifty!" He then turned toward me and yelled into my face, "I could throw rocks down there and hit that many! You are a major screw up, aren't you!" "Yes, Drill Sergeant," I yelled back. "Everyone else is going to get a pass to go into town this weekend, but you are staying behind to pull K.P. all weekend. Do you like that?" "Yes, Drill Sergeant," I yelled again. I could feel tears starting to well up but I was determined to not let him see me cry. "Get out of here. I'm sick of looking at you!" "Yes, Drill Sergeant," I yelled. I gave a sharp salute and fell back in to the formation.

Later, in the barracks, my fellow soldiers all said, "Why didn't you tell him your glasses were broken and you couldn't see the targets?" "He already knew that, " I explained, "he just didn't care." I knew he had tried his best to break my spirit. But I also knew -- he did not succeed.

I may have regretted my lazy ways, but some habits are hard to break. One day, when the duties were assigned at our barracks, I found out I had lawn detail. I remembered those days back home when I got out of mowing the lawn by paying somebody off. Here in the Army there would be none of that. I took a look at this huge lawn that I was supposed to mow. It looked the size of a football field. I trudged over to the supply area and said I was reporting to pick up a lawn mower. The sergeant pointed to his right and there was a push mower, the last one in the whole company. No engine. I was to be the engine.

I wheeled the mower outside and headed toward the never-ending blades of grass awaiting me. I could tell this would be an all-day project that I desperately wanted to avoid. Then I spied a large rock partially hidden by the tall grass. "This is my only chance," I thought. I headed the mower toward this jagged rock at full speed. Wham! I smashed into the rock once and pulled the mower back to survey the damage. The rock had done its job. The mower was now beyond repair. I felt a little guilty but it had to be done. I dragged the sickly mower back to the supply area. The sergeant looked up from his paperwork and growled, "What're you back here for already?" I said, "There's something wrong with this mower." He took a quick look at it and pointing to his right said, "Stick it over there." I did, and was about to leave when I heard him say, "Here." I turned to look as he handed me a sickle. "Oh my God, I'll never finish now," I said to myself. I took the instrument from his hand and walked outside, pondering how I would be able to get out of this mess.

There was only one thing to do. I found the same big rock and I swung the sickle against it with all my might. Wham! I headed back to the supply area, thinking to myself, "I hope this works. If he hands me a fingernail clipper, I'm doomed." As I walked in, he saw me and said, "Don't tell me you broke the sickle too!" I started to explain, but he just raised his hand and said, "Just put it over there and get out of here!" I laid it by the broken mower and left quickly. I can't say I felt smug that I'd gotten away with something. I truly felt I had dodged a bullet this time and I probably wouldn't be this lucky again.

Another thing happened a few weeks later that would signal the end of my trying to avoid responsibility. After firing our weapons at the rifle range, I hated having to clean the weapon. We had to run an oily rag down the barrel and then take it to the drill sergeant who would inspect it. Invariably it was never clean enough. I would take it back time and again until after several tries it would finally pass. I hated it. So I came up with a scheme.

I knew that there was about a hundred men in our squadron but only 50 places at the firing range, so we always were split up into two groups. Firing order one and firing order two. I took one of my fellow soldiers aside and offered a proposition. He would make sure he got into the first firing order and I would make sure to be in the second. As soon as he finished firing, he would walk past me and hand me his weapon. I would then fire his rifle instead of mine. When we got back to the barracks, mine would still be clean and I could simply run an oily rag down the barrel one time and it would immediately pass. For this privilege I would pay him $10. Finding he liked the idea, I didn't see how this plan could fail.

That day at the range all went as planned. He got set up in the first order and I was in the second. I left my rifle sitting to the side. As he came back, we both glanced around to make sure no one would see, and then he handed his rifle to me. "This is brilliant," I thought as I headed to the front of the line. There was just one minor problem I had not anticipated. Before you are allowed on the firing line, the First Sergeant has to make sure there is not a "live round" in your rifle. He determines this by running a metal rod down the barrel of the weapon and then declares it "clear." To do this, he grabs hold of the muzzle of the weapon with his left hand and inserts the rod with his right.

Under normal circumstances, this is perfectly fine. But I am now carrying a weapon that has just recently been fired. That means the muzzle is *still hot*. As the sergeant grabbed my rifle, he jerked his left hand away and yelled, "How did that weapon get so hot?" He was glowering at me and I could feel my heart stop. "If he finds out what I've done," I said to myself, "I'll be cleaning every weapon in this entire company!" -- "It must have been in the hot sun, Drill Sergeant!" I stammered. He stared me straight in the eye. I could tell he wasn't buying this lame explanation, but he had no way to refute it either. "Get up to the line," he bellowed. I walked to the front of the firing line with my knees shaking. I knew I would never again try to outsmart the system. I had learned a valuable lesson that day, one I would never forget.

I was quickly learning that basic was not all bad. There were moments when it seemed even the drill sergeants had a sense of humor. I first noticed this when we were on bivouac. We were to stay out in the field and sleep in tents for two weeks. The first night in the field the sergeant said, "Before you go to sleep, take a big stick and beat it around inside your

101

tent!" So we said, "Why should be do that, Drill Sergeant?" He said, "That's to get rid of the 'No-Shoulders.'" "What's a 'No-Shoulders?'" we asked. He said, "A snake. You ever see a snake with shoulders?" He then proceeded to explain that in the training session before ours they found a trainee dead in his tent from snakebite. Yes, I'll sleep real well tonight, thanks for the bedtime story, Drill Sergeant.

The funniest thing occurred a week after that. We were standing in formation when the drill sergeant announced, "I need some volunteers." I had always heard not to volunteer, but I figured the odds would be in my favor. They'd see that I was a team player and probably pick someone else. I raised my hand and noticed I was the only one with my hand up. "Private Corey, get up here," he yelled. As I ran for the platform, I couldn't help but think," I'm really in for it now," and prepared myself for who-knows-what's coming next. The sergeant said, "Have a seat here, Corey," as he pulled up a folding chair. I sat down and he said, "Are you comfortable?" I nodded and said, "Yes, Drill Sergeant." I was being very cautious now; it wasn't like these guys to be kind. Something was coming and I wasn't sure what. "Have some Kool-Aid," he said as he handed me a small plastic cup filled with red liquid. "That's it," I thought to myself. "They're probably giving me poisoned Kool-Aid and they'll all stand around laughing and watch me writhe and die." I took a sip of the drink and he said, "How's that taste -- pretty good?" I nodded politely and said, "Yes, Drill Sergeant," but thought to myself, "Please, just get on with it, the suspense is killing me."

Are You Talking To Me?

The drill sergeant turned away from me and addressed the troops still standing in formation, "You know, there's an old saying, 'It doesn't pay to volunteer in the Army.' Well, Corey here volunteered and *he's* sitting in the shade drinking Kool-Aid. The rest of you a**holes get down and give me fifty pushups!" He then turned to me...and smiled. This was the first time I had ever seen him smile and I figured it'd probably be the last. I smiled back, knowing I had dodged a bullet. I finished my drink as the rest of the troops finished their pushups. He then yelled, "The next time I ask for volunteers I want to see a *lot* of hands instead of just one!" He turned and said, "O.K. Corey, you can fall back in." The rest of the guys glared at me, but they knew it was just one of those things. I lucked out that time and they didn't.

ELEVEN

November of 1968, I had just returned home 11 days before my 19th birthday. I was glad to be home from the ordeal of basic training and no more being yelled at by drill sergeants. My desire to be on the radio had not decreased. If anything, I wanted it now even more than before. But it seemed too much like a dream -- a dream too high to reach.

I felt I had to take my quest to a whole new level. I convinced my father to enroll me in the Columbia School of Broadcasting. By now he could see that this desire of mine was not going away any time soon. I guess he figured, what the heck, this'll be cheaper than paying for four years of college. Whatever thoughts were on his mind, he agreed. This was a big step for me, but a peculiar one. This course was to be done via the mail. Yes, I was to take an *announcing* course by sending in a tape recording of my voice reading a script. My instructor would then mail back my original tape, along with a critique tape. This was to continue for a period of about two years. My hope was that when I graduated, their placement service would get me on a small radio station somewhere, then I could work my way back to St. Louis to end up at the place I *really* wanted to be -- KSHE Radio. When you really want something and you take the first step toward it, God can intervene for you. He can provide a miracle. This is exactly what was about to occur even though I had no idea it would happen the way it did.

On December 24, 1968, I was asleep in my bedroom at about 9:00 in the morning. My dad opened my bedroom door to wake me. "Donald, there's somebody on the phone for you." I thought, "Who in the world is calling me at this hour on Christmas Eve?" I asked, "Who is it?" Dad replied, "I think he's from KSHE Radio." Oh my God -- was I awake then! I jumped out of bed and grabbed the phone. Shaking with anticipation, but trying to sound as professional as possible, I said, "Hello?"

The guy didn't beat around the bush. "Can you come in this morning and work?" he said. Without a second's hesitations, I said, "I'll be there in fifteen minutes." I wasn't kidding either. I threw on some clothes and made a mad dash to my car. It took less than 15 minutes. At that point I was not even thinking, "This could be my big chance." I was really running on autopilot. When he said to come in and work, for all I knew I'd be sweeping the floor. I didn't care. All I knew was that I was going to be working at the radio station I had dreamed about ever since I first heard it.

When I arrived, he escorted me to the control room.

Now I was really getting excited. Unless he was taking me there to sweep the floor, which was doubtful, I was actually going to be on the air. This was it. This was my shot at the big time. I was to go on from 10 a.m. to 1p.m. There was already a record playing on one of the turntables as the fellow turned to me and posed this question: "Have you ever 'run a board' before?"

Now I'm in a sticky situation. I had used mixers before, but nothing like this one. It had dozens of knobs and switches and looked like the instrument panel you see in the cockpit of an airplane. So, have I run a board before? Not like this. Not on your life. But what if I say, "No." Maybe he'll say, "O.K., never mind, we'll get somebody else," and escort me out. To answer his question I simply replied, "Sure."

I sat down in the chair as he quickly gave me some instructions. "This switch turns your mike on and off. Once the mike is on, the speakers are muted and you'll have to listen in these headphones. This is turntable one, this is turntable two and this is tape machine number one..." He rattled on like this for several minutes as I tried to take it all in. I made particular note of the two turntable controls and the microphone switch. Lucky for me, there were just one or two commercials scheduled within the first hour. If I could just play a few records until I got the feel of it, maybe it would be all right.

I picked out an album and placed it onto the empty turntable. I lifted the tone arm to put the stylus on the record, but my hand was shaking so badly it looked like I had an uncontrollable tremor in my right arm and hand. The guy looked at me and said, "Am I making you nervous?" I said, "Uh, no, I'm always like this." He said, "If you need me, I'll be right down the hall." I thanked him, and after he left I cued up the record and waited until the current song ended. I hit the start switch and turned up the volume, while quickly turning down the other. It worked. I had gone from one song to another and it sounded pretty smooth. I did this until 10 a.m. It was now time for what is known in the business as the "Legal I.D." This is where you say the station's call letters, and the city in which the tower is located. Which meant I would have to open the microphone and actually speak my first words on a real radio station.

It was the moment I had anticipated for years, but now that it was upon me I was scared. "It's just one little sentence," I thought to myself. One sentence it may have been, but the feeling was like giving a speech to a room full of people. I may have been the only one in that room, but I knew -- there's a lot people listening out there.

As I put on the headphones and turned on the microphone switch, the last of the record faded away to silence. I took a quick breath and said, "This is K-S-H-E -- Crestwood, Missouri." I started another record and fell back in the chair feeling like I'd just had a near miss with a truck. But when the moment had passed, I said to myself, "*I think I can do this!*" From that point on, it got a little easier each time I spoke. By the time 1 p.m. arrived, I thought, "I hope the other DJ doesn't get here. I could do this all day!" I found out later that my father had called everyone we knew and told them I was on the radio. Thank God I didn't know; I was nervous enough as it was.

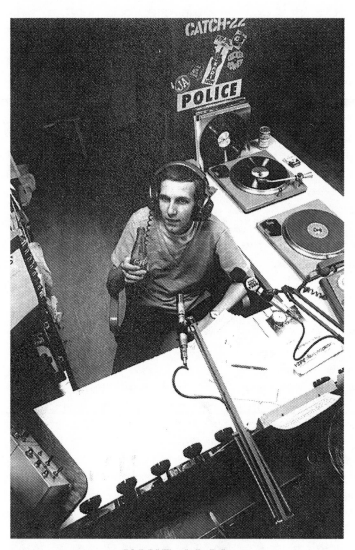

KSHE 1969

Don Corey

I remember virtually nothing about that first broadcast; I was far too excited and nervous. It must have gone all right though, because they asked me to come back again. I was scheduled weekends, the shift experienced by all beginning DJs, and I was thrilled to do it. I would get whatever hours no one else wanted, which was fine with me. I still can recall the thrill of stopping out to the station and looking on the corkboard-covered wall in the studio. That's where the schedule was posted. I would look at it like students look for their final exam scores. My hope: my name would be on the weekend schedule.

One of the interesting things about working for KSHE was one of the perks, namely "groupies." I had always heard about these girls who were wild about musicians in rock bands, but I had no idea that there were radio groupies too. I soon found out, much to my delight. When I was in high school, I used to joke that "I couldn't charm an old maid out of a burning building." That may have been an exaggeration -- but not by much. The girls in school all went for the "jocks," mainly the football players. Some of the girls even went for the highly intellectual types. I did not fit any of these categories. It was so bad that I didn't even fit in with "the geeks." But all this changed as soon as I was an on-the-air personality. Suddenly girls called *me*! Although not prepared for this, it certainly didn't take me long to adjust. Girls would call and tell me how much they enjoyed my show and what a beautiful voice I had. Man, this was as close to heaven as this kid had been on earth yet. I suddenly went from having only one girlfriend to having several at one time.

There was a downside though. Sometimes it was hard to keep them straight. I remember one embarrassing situation. I answered the request line and the voice on the other end said, "Hi Don! It's *me*." So I said, "Yeah, how're you doing?" And she said, "Are we going out again soon?" I said, "Uh, well, probably, I'll have to see what's going on this weekend. She said, "You don't know who this is, do you?" The way she said it, she sounded as though I had damn well better know who this is. I tried to ad-lib out of it by saying, "How's your cat?" A lot of the girls I went out with had cats, maybe this would give me a clue to which girl this was without having to ask her name. "I don't have a cat!" she said angrily as she hung up the phone. Oh well, I blew that one.

Considering my early dating life, I was always sympathetic to anyone who had trouble meeting and dating good-looking women. There was one memorable instance when I visited the General Grant Colonial Village Apartments. They had a very nice swimming pool for the residents to use.

I was hanging out poolside, enjoying the day, when a young man who lived there came up to me with an odd request. He really wanted to meet an exceptionally pretty girl that always came around to swim and suntan, but was too shy to ask her out. I asked him what he had in mind. He had a plan. He would invite the girl and me back to his apartment. Once there, he would give each of us a soda and some snacks. Then I was to suddenly remember I had somewhere I needed to go, so the two of them would be alone and he could get to know her better.

Don Corey

Always on the lookout to do a good deed, I agreed to do it. A few minutes later the three of us were headed off to his abode.

When we got inside, he went to the kitchen to get our sodas. The girl and I sat together on his sofa. It felt a little awkward at this point, because I wasn't sure if I should strike up a conversation or not. After all, this was going to be his little get-together, not mine. I wasn't going to be there for very long, if his plan worked the way he'd anticipated.

What I did not know was, this little party was about to take a weird turn. Unbeknownst to me, or the girl, this guy had a pet parakeet. This would not have posed a problem, except for the fact that he had chosen to let it out of its cage. I have no idea why. Suddenly this bird comes flying across the room at warp speed, heading right toward this poor innocent girl's face! She ducked her head as it went flying by. She turned to me and said, "What the hell was that?" I shrugged my shoulders and said, "Uh, I guess he's got a pet parakeet." She stood up. "I'm outta here," she said as she headed for the door.

The guy came walking back in with two sodas and said, "Where is she?" I said, "She left -- you need to get rid of that bird."

Girls would fall in love with my voice on the radio. The problem with that--- what happens when we met in person and the voice doesn't match the body? Most of my dates were fairly gracious when this occurred. But one time it didn't go well at all. I had talked to this girl on the request line several nights in a row, and she said she wanted to meet me in person. She told me her address and we decided to hook up on the following Saturday at about 7 p.m.

Saturday came. I dressed up in a suit and tie, got myself properly spiffed up with a hint of cologne. I found the address and walked up the sidewalk, wondering what this girl was going to look like. I knocked and the door swung open wide. The girl was exceptionally beautiful -- better than I had anticipated. I was thinking, "Man, I won the lottery this time." But then she looked at me and said, "I changed my mind." She shut the door. I stood there for a moment -- silently trying to grasp what had happened. It hurt. I turned around and went back home -- trying to remind myself about that stupid old line about "other fish in the sea." Right now, I didn't care about the other fish. I needed a hug.

Strange coincidences always happen in my life. Most of them were relatively ordinary -- whimsical and odd, but never bizarre. That would all change. Since I worked the midnight shift, my schedule was quite different from everyone else, which was fine with me. I'd never been a "morning person," so working at night suited me just fine. The only drawback was trying to sleep during the day. I had black cardboard covering the windows and a sign by my front door that read, "Do not ring doorbell until after 3 p.m. I would get home at about 6:30 in the morning and "hit the sack" about 7. That meant I'd get a full eight hours sleep and get up at about 3.

This particular day I went to sleep at the usual time, but was awakened after about 90 minutes with a horrible nightmare. In this dream, I was on my way to my friend Tom's house in Chesterfield. I was on Highway 244 going north, when I felt the car pulling to the right. I pulled to the shoulder of the road just before the Manchester exit. When I got out to see what was wrong, I saw that my rear tire on the passenger side was flat. I got out the spare tire and used the jack that I always kept in the trunk for emergencies. I removed the lug nuts and once the wheel was high enough off the ground, I reached into the wheel well to remove the tire. At this point in the dream, a big semi-truck went by and the car fell off the jack and crushed both of my arms! This jolted me awake, gasping for air. The dream seemed so real, I was pretty shaken, but I knew I had to get back to sleep. I got up and grabbed a quick drink of soda and went back to bed.

Strangely, as frightening as the dream was, when I finally woke up, I did not remember it at all. I got ready to head out because my friend Tom had invited me over to his bootleg radio station where we were going to try out some new equipment he had purchased. I got in the car and drove the usual route, which included going north on Highway 244. I had only gone a short distance when the car seemed to pull to the right. To this day, for reasons I will never understand, I still did not remember the dream I had, only hours before.

Almost reaching the Manchester exit, I pulled onto the right shoulder and stopped the car. I got out to see what was wrong. The rear tire on the passenger side was completely flat. It must have been a pretty fast leak; I guess I had run over a nail. I opened the trunk and pulled out the jack. I jacked up the car and took the lug nuts off the wheel. I was just starting to reach into the wheel well when I heard a huge truck heading my way in the next lane. As I felt the ground shake under me, I thought to myself, "This seems familiar somehow..." Suddenly I remembered the dream!

I jumped back just as the car fell, pinning the jack underneath! Looking at this in total amazement, I felt a queasy feeling in the pit of my stomach. No way was I going to try to get that jack out from under the car.

I decided to walk to the nearest filling station, which was just down Manchester. I explained what had happened and a nice man drove me back to my car in the station's tow truck. When we arrived at the scene, he used his jack and had just extricated my jack when another truck came rumbling by and -- boom! -- The car fell down again and pinned his jack underneath! Of course by now, I was completely freaked out. It didn't seem to bother him that much. I guess he was used to this kind of thing, but I wasn't going anywhere near the car until this whole ordeal was over. He used my jack to remove his, and then he replaced the tire and put the lug nuts back on. I gave him a nice big tip and thanked him profusely. He got in his tow truck and drove away.

As for me, I decided not to go to Tom's after all, and headed home. I called to tell him I was sorry to cancel our meeting, but the whole thing had me pretty frazzled. Why didn't I remember the dream until the last minute? How could I dream something hours before it actually happens in the exact spot and the exact way I had visualized? Was this some kind of sign from God? Do I have to worry, every time I have a dream that it's going to come true like this one? There was no easy answer to any of these questions. One thing I did know. This life of mine, which had always been a little strange, had just become a lot more peculiar.

TWELVE

One of my very first experiences when I started working weekends happened on Sundays. I engineered a program for a guy named Eric, who had an early morning show called, "The Continental and German Music Program." This was a leftover from the days before KSHE became a rock station.

The station originally was in the basement of a guy named Ed Ceries. They played songs by the likes of Les and Larry Elgart, Ernie Heckshire and the Fabulous Fairmont Orchestra, Ted Heath and Lester Lanin. Supposedly this Eric fellow's contract with the old KSHE had not yet run out. So there I was, running the board for him. He brought in his own records, polkas and waltzes. The craziest part of it all was -- he spoke German. Not an occasional word, everything he said was German. All I could do was sit there and make sure the volume on his microphone was correct and start the records for him. When the mike was off he would tell me in English which cuts on the album to cue up, but as soon as that mike came on it was "back to Germany."

I reminded him that when he wanted me to start the record, he had to "point to me." Otherwise, he might well be saying, "And now here's such and such song," but all I heard was gibberish. Too often, he would stop speaking, and then look at me as if to say, "Well, are you going to start the record or not?" That was when I'd hit the start switch, turn off his mike and say, "Eric, remember, you have to point." He'd say, "Yes, I remember now. Sorry." It was like being in a car with someone who is driving, but you're the one giving directions. Turn left here; turn right there. But soon you just sit there as they go flying past the street and you think, "why didn't they turn?"

The funny thing was when the request line would ring. When I answered the phone, it would be one of two different scenarios. The person on the other end would be speaking German, so I'd hurriedly hand the phone to Eric, or regular KSHE listeners would ask, "What in the world is this weird stuff you're playing?" and I'd have to explain to them to tune back in around noon to hear the normal rock format.

A third scenario was when a regular listener would ask, "Can you play some Rolling Stones?" Yeah, that'd fit in just great between the waltz and the polka.

Sometimes I'd hang around after my shift was over on Sunday and talk to the guy who came on the air after me. One of these guys was Michael Charles. He was a complete riot! Personally I thought he'd be better suited to television, because some of his facial expressions were just hysterical and were completely lost on the radio audience. He would do the strangest things. For one, he looked like he might have come from another planet. His hair always looked the same. He might have been an android for all I knew, but he was a funny android if he was one.

His announcing style was very interesting, always speaking in hushed tones, very authoritative, like he knew something deeply important that no one else knew. He had a very serious sound. That is what makes something he did next so darn funny.

When his song ran out, he keyed up the microphone and said, in his usual serious voice, "I have a note here from the management." He rattled a piece of paper to make his point more clear. "It says, 'Dear Michael, you always sound so serious when you speak. In the future, please try to sound a little more like a disc jockey.'" Then he paused and said, "Well...O.K." He then completely changed his voice, tempo and volume and said- "HEY, IT'S SIXTY FIVE BIG DEGREES ON THE BIG 95 KAAAAY-SHEEE-NINETEEEE-FIIIIVE!" He said this in that radically spastic sounding voice you hear from car commercial guys. He then turned off the microphone and laughed like a deranged man. For my part I was so astonished at this metamorphosis, for a moment I couldn't believe my ears. Then I busted out laughing right along with him. He had a funny look on his face as if to say, "I pulled one over on them that time!"

On the same show, he had a record playing on the

air, but he had the volume down on the studio monitor. What this means is, although the record is playing on everyone's radio, neither of us could hear it...DJs do this sometimes so they can talk on the phone, or maybe it's a song they don't like. Anyway, he had the volume down and the request lines were all lit up like crazy, but he was ignoring them because the two of us were talking. I don't know why, but I suddenly got the feeling something was not quite right. Early on a Sunday morning, there were usually not a lot of phone calls. So I asked him, "What song are you playing?" Mike replied, "It's 'Toad' by Cream." I asked, "How long a song is it?" He said, "It's 5:09. Why?" I said, "'Cause it's been playing for 10 minutes!" Mike turned up the monitor and, sure enough, the record had been skipping for the last five minutes! The lines were lighting up to try to tell him his song was stuck. Mike immediately had a plan. The record was on the farthest turntable away, so he told me to get ready. As soon as he keyed the microphone, he would quickly turn down the album, and then I was to pick up the tonearm and move it ahead just slightly. He motioned to me as he keyed his microphone. In his most official sounding voice he said, "You've been listening to the *extended version* of "Toad," by the Cream." He then turned off the microphone and once again we both laughed ourselves silly. He was a funny guy and I really liked his style. He just didn't seem to fit on KSHE. But I guess that was his charm.

Sometimes on Sunday mornings instead of Michael, or the Continental and German Music Program, they would have a pre-recorded show. It was a syndicated religious program. It consisted of a roundtable discussion with several different speakers. All I had to do was put on the tape and let it roll. So there I sat, just making sure the volume was right and to be ready in case the tape broke. Frankly, I thought the whole program was rather boring -- although sometimes the panel of "experts" would get into heated arguments about who was right. This was the only bright spot in the show as far as I was concerned.

It did give me an idea though -- although I never acted on it for fear of being fired. What I really wanted to do was take the tape and edit it. Right at the part where the panel members were reaching the crescendo of their arguing, I would splice in gunshots. Bang! Bang! Bang! Followed by complete silence... Then I would simply come on the air and say, "This has been a public service presentation." What a riot! Needless to say I never did it, but I always thought it would have been hysterical.

After working my fair share of weekends, I landed a regular permanent shift. Midnight to 6. This turned out to be my favorite time slot, because I had a lot more latitude in what I could do. I was free to play pretty much anything I wanted to, as long as the album was there in the studio. Also, there were very few commercials during that time period, just public service announcements and the occasional newscast.

Only on the air in this late-night shift for less than a week, something frightening happened. About three o'clock in the morning, a light on the back control rack lit up. It was labeled "EBS Alert" which stood for Emergency Broadcast System. No one had ever pointed this out to me, nor had anyone bothered to tell me what to do if it came on. But there it was. I figured, of course this must be one of those "tests" you hear on the radio from time to time. But why in the world would they run an EBS test at 3 a.m.? What if it isn't a test, but an actual emergency? I let the record continue to play while I ran to the transmitter room to check the Associated Press news machine. Nothing.

I ran back to the studio and looked out the window to see if there were any rockets flying through Crestwood. No rockets. I thought for a moment, if there really is an emergency and I'm just sitting here playing Bob Dylan on the radio -- well, that's not a good thing. On the other hand, if I stop the record and say this is an emergency, and it isn't, then I panic the entire St. Louis area and I'll probably get fired. So I did what I considered to be the most logical thing to do. I let Bob Dylan continue.

At 6 a.m. when the next DJ came in, I ran up to him and said, "Man, am I glad you're here!" I told him what had happened and he just smiled and stepped over to the rack where the EBS light was still on. Balling his left hand into a fist, he struck the side of the cabinet. Bam! The EBS light went off. "That happens sometimes," he said dryly.

In March of 1970, the KSHE secretaries informed me that Meramec College was looking for a Master of Ceremonies for a variety show they were planning. They told me I would probably not get paid for this gig. I figured, what the heck, I needed to get used to doing public speaking. Being in that control room by myself was all well and good, but this would be my first chance to see how I did in front of a crowd. Besides, these will be college-age kids, so it should be a breeze.

Agreeing to do it, I met with the staff of the Meramec Choir. The program would be called the "Campus After Dark Variety Show." There would be about seven different acts, followed by an intermission, and then another seven acts followed by a finale. My job was to introduce each act. If I wanted, I could throw in a few one-liners to liven things up. This sounded just fine to me. The show would be presented on March 19 and 20 at 8p.m. at the Meramec Campus.

When everyone was in place, I eagerly ran onstage and enthusiastically presented myself as being from KSHE radio and introduced the first act. They were the Quarter Tones consisting of Mike on trumpet, Ken on guitar, Jack on drums and Gail as the vocalist. When they finished their musical interlude and the applause died down, I complimented them on their performance and then threw out my first "one-liner" of the evening.

It fell further than flat. If there had been a basement, that's where it would have fallen. It was so quiet you could hear the quiet hum of the fluorescent lights. This was all the more disconcerting considering the applause that had just gone before this silence. They liked the music -- they didn't like the joke.

Nonetheless, I consider myself a professional; so I sucked it up and went on to introduce the next two acts, the Top 30 Meramec Singers and Blufolk. Once again both of these acts were received with thunderous applause. As the clapping subsided, I again commented on the music and threw out what I thought was a very funny ad-lib. Nothing. There was no sound whatsoever -- no crickets, no coughing. It was eerie. But now, as though it couldn't get any worse, two guys in the front row actually heckled me! They said stuff like, "Yeah, that's funny." "That's a good one." "Ha- ha."

I suddenly understood the phrase that comedians use when they say they "died" on stage. This was worse than death -- more like torture. Again, I maintained my composure. I smiled, and introduced the next acts, knowing I just had four more before the intermission. "If I can just hold out that long," I thought to myself.

After each act was through I tried my best to get the audience to respond, but they would have none of it. When the intermission finally arrived, I explained that during the break there would be refreshments at a snack area. Then I said, "I may or may not be back. I may have to go out and get loaded. But feel free to return after the intermission and we'll see what happens."

Then I went back behind the stage and sat down in a small chair to look quietly at my notes. I wondered how I possibly could have stumbled into this thorny mess. I'm not even getting paid for this. Why is the audience so hostile? My jokes can't be that bad! Deep in the midst of feeling sorry for myself, two guys came around the corner and said, "Don Corey?" I looked up and said, "Yes?" The two guys said, "We're your two hecklers from the front row. We just wanted to let you know it's all in good fun." They stepped forward and extended their hands for me to give them each a handshake.

I was completely taken aback. As I shook their hands, I asked, "Are you serious?" They said it was a trick that they do. They have an agreement with the rest of the crowd. No matter what this guy does, don't laugh and don't applaud. Just sit there. They said it's something they like to do to see how the MC handles it. They said most people get really hostile and retaliate. My reaction though, was to be cordial and not act upset. They told me not to worry, that after the intermission it would be "a whole new ballgame." Well, I just had to laugh. We talked for a few minutes about what it was like to be on KSHE, and then it was time to go back on stage for the second half of the show. The two guys went back out front and, true to their word, as soon as I threw out another little quip, the audience cheered and laughed. What a relief this was! And what a blessing! In that very evening I got to experience the awful feeling of bombing on stage without having to really bomb. I will never forget the gift they gave me that night.

Although I spent most of my days at KSHE on the midnight shift, I did go through a short period where I recorded commercials. This was due in large part to a man named Al Leeges. He felt that it was a shame that everyone else at the station got a crack at commercials while I got left out entirely. So August of 1970, I was happy to be included in the task of going into the production room and recording "spots" for clients.

Don Corey

The names of some of these will give an idea of the things going on at that time. The Prodigal Son at 8860 Ladue Road, billed as an "Artisan Center and Head Shop," sold posters, jewelry and other miscellaneous items. There was The Cauldron, an "occult shop" at 4005 Gravois, advertised as "owned and operated by a witch." Post Bellum at 219 S. Florissant Road featured authentic Indian and Afghanistan incense. The inventory of Nirvana at 1341 20th Street in Granite City included leather products and bumper stickers. Cachorka, 6380 Delmar in University City sold jewelry, posters, pipes and leather goods -- "the unusual at reasonable prices." A store called Grand Sun billed itself as "a head shop now in Festus," was located at 104 South Second Street and sold record albums for only $3.50. That wasn't the only bargain. Back then you could see Grand Funk Railroad and Humble Pie at the Kiel Auditorium for -- get this -- $3.50, 4.50 and $5.50 a seat. Hard to believe, isn't it?

One of the crazy things about going in to do "production" was the fact that a lot of these clients liked to write their own advertisements. This could sometimes be a problem. Let's face it. If writing an effective ad was easy, everybody would be doing it. On more than a few occasions, a client thought he had a really good piece of copy and we'd have to gently try to persuade him to change it. After all, we wanted his ad to bring in lots of business for him.

I remember one guy in particular who had the word "groovy" sprinkled throughout his commercial. I tried to explain that the word "groovy" had gone out of vogue almost as fast as it came in. But he said no, he wanted it left in because, as he put it, "I know what's hip to these kids." Oh well.

A funny thing happened one time with a commercial for a place called Charlie's Chicken. The sponsor wanted two people to read the copy -- a girl and a guy. I was the guy and one of our receptionists was to be the girl. The two of us went into the production studio to record the commercial. It should have been simple enough; it was just a 30-second spot. But the sponsor wanted the sound of "a chicken clucking in the background." Why this was important was completely lost on us, but what the sponsor wanted, the sponsor got.

I found a sound effects record with a chicken clucking and cued it up on the turntable. The girl and I held the copy in front of us and began to read. The copy was written by the client and consisted of a large smattering of words beginning with the letters, "ch." That is, one of the lines went, "Why is Charlie's Chicken so chewy, Chester?" Trying to read each line with several of these "ch" words without messing up, and hearing that chicken cluck-cluck-clucking- was almost too much.

We were having a difficult time getting through it without breaking up. One take I would get almost all the way through and she would laugh. Then she'd get right to the end and I'd lose it. We had done dozens of takes and soon we were getting so hysterical that we couldn't get past the first sentence without laughing like idiots! To make matters worse, the very last part of the commercial went like this:

Don Corey

"Charlie's Chicken- it's just like Grandma used to make."
"Oh, Grandma never cooked chicken."
"Why not, Chester?"
"Grandma was a bookie."

Well I'd get to that very last line and I just could not get it out! We laughed and laughed until our sides ached. I finally told her, "We're never going to finish at this rate. There's only one thing we can do." I decided we would record our parts "bare voice" and add the clucking chicken later. It was still hard getting through it, but we would just say a line at a time and then I spliced the segments together and over-dubbed the chicken.

The commercial didn't run very long and I have no idea how many customers it brought in, but I'll never forget the hilarity of trying to record it. I wish now I had the "out-takes."

Shortly after that, Charlie's Chicken clucked its last.

Perhaps you've had a dream that goes something like this: You're back in High School and you're late for class. You can't find the right room or you can't find your locker. Most people have had this dream or a variation of it. Guess what? There is a disc jockey version of this.

Radio stations have two important logs. A transmitter log contains meter readings, taken every half hour. The other log contains the PSA's and commercials and what time they are run. The commercials are very important because they allow a station to stay on the air and in the black. These spots must be run exactly when scheduled, plus or minus 15 minutes. Affidavits are signed stating that the commercials aired at the correct times and if not, the station must do a "make good."

In my dream I am back on KSHE during my usual shift. Things are not going smoothly at all. Albums that I want to play aren't there, only empty jackets. The live copy is missing. Records run out before I can cue another one. Then to my horror, I suddenly notice I haven't run any commercials for two hours! I begin to panic, then wake up in a cold sweat and realize it was that nightmare again. It's the same every time, but it seems so real, I can't tell it's a dream until I wake up.

Apparently I'm not the only one. At a party I mentioned the dream to some other DJs and they said they have the same recurring dream! It must be some sort of DJ curse.

THIRTEEN

It was May of 1970. I wanted to keep my new Pontiac Lemans looking great. Having heard good things about the gentleness of a new car wash that had just opened up on Watson Road, the General Grant Car Wash, I headed right over. I liked it right away, because you could look through several large windows and watch the machines doing their thing as your car rolled along. When my car exited the wash, a couple of guys waited outside to wipe the car down, inside and out. This was an added plus and the guys did a wonderful job. The car looked great. One of the young men noticed that I had several KSHE bumper stickers all over my car and asked, "Do you work for KSHE or something?" I said, "How'd you guess?" He laughed and said, "One of these days I'm going to work there." I wished him well and said if there's anything I can do to help you, let me know. His name was Mark Klose.

Don Corey

Life is funny that way. Sure enough, a couple of years later he came to KSHE and, of course, the rest is history. The funny thing about this is that Mark was the very first employee to be hired when the car wash first opened its doors. The owner, Rich Barthelmass, was quite impressed with this young man. When I later talked with him about Mark, Rich said he was happy that he got to pursue his dream, but sad to lose such a good worker. Years later Mark said, "I guess at that point I wasn't much of a businessman. I left the car wash making $150 a week, to join KSHE at $25 a week!"

That's the price you pay to follow your dream sometimes. But Mark is still out there, on the air and doing the fine job he's always been known for.

I've known Mark Klose and "Radio Rich" Dalton a long time. They are two of the finest, most down-to-earth guys you will ever meet. My hat is off to anyone who can remain in such a quickly changing environment and still be at the top of his game after all these years. The knowledge both of these guys have about music is incredible. It was an honor just to work in the same arena they did.

Rich and his son, Rick, still run the General Grant Car Wash, which is still where everyone should go. It's without question the finest car wash around with one of the best greeting card selections in town. The staff is always courteous and professional. And, no, I did not receive any promotional consideration for this. It's simply the truth.

By August of 1970 another new challenge would come my way. KSHE was promoting live broadcasts from clubs in the St. Louis area with Ron Lipe (a.k.a. Prince Knight) as the M.C. Clubs like the Rainy Daze at 14100 Olive Street Road and the Music Palace at 9765 St. Charles Rock Road were popular in those days. A new club, just opened, was trying to get established so live broadcasts were planned. The name of the club was The Spiral Staircase on Chambers Road. The Prince, already booked with a full calendar, asked me if I would be interested in doing some live remotes on Monday nights. I told him quite frankly that although I was flattered to be asked, I was very much concerned about how well I would do in front of a live audience. After all, it had been just five months since my Meramec College debacle and although that turned out all right, I was quite sure that a nightclub audience would not be as forgiving. Besides, there is a very big difference between being on a stage at a college campus and being in front of an audience, and on the radio at the same time. Nevertheless, the Prince assured me that it wasn't as bad as all that. He said, "When those bright lights come on, you can't see the audience anyway. You'll be fine." I seriously had my doubts, but this was an opportunity that I didn't want to pass up. He told me he would come out with me on the Monday before, and introduce me. That calmed me a little, so I agreed.

Monday, August 17 Prince Knight introduced me on stage and I got a brief taste of how the remote would work. About 15 minutes before the remote was to begin, Prince warmed up the crowd. He asked some trivia questions about rock music and gave away albums to whoever came up with the correct answer. At the top of the hour, the show would be broadcast live on KSHE. A local band would play and Prince would do his announcements between songs, telling everyone to "come on down and join in the fun." I was still a little frightened at the prospect of doing this all by myself, but I had already committed to it and I'm a man of my word.

The next Monday rolled around and it was time for my first remote broadcast. I got a stack of albums from the station to be used as give-aways, packed them in my car and headed for Chambers Road. As I was driving along, I memorized some things I could say just in case I got stage fright. It was raining that night, so I thought I could open up by saying, "Thanks for coming in out of the rain to be here for our live broadcast," or something along those lines. I arrived at the venue and gave the albums to the bartender for safe keeping until I was ready for them. I then made sure the audio hookups were in place, did a mike check and verified that my watch was synchronized to the station's clock. I thought to myself, maybe this won't be so bad after all.

It would actually be worse. At about 15 before the hour, I prepared to warm up the crowd as the Prince had done. I went up to the bar to get the stack of albums, but the guy supposedly holding them wasn't around. Instead, there was a girl I had never met. So I said, "Hey, I need that stack of albums over there." She shot me a look of disgust and said, "Those records are for the deejay." I said, "I *am the deejay!*" I guess I didn't look the part. This was my first hint things were about to get ugly.

I took my stack of albums and climbed onto the

stage. People were already coming in and it looked like a pretty full crowd. I had hoped the rain would have kept them away. No such luck. The spotlight came on. Prince was only partly right. With that bright spotlight, I could not make out any discernable faces, but I could certainly tell there was a crowd out there. I tried to calm the panicky feeling welling up from my midsection. My heartbeat pounded in my eardrums like a primitive tribal beat straight from Hell itself. I tried to remember the things I had memorized, but my brain was swirling around and arguing with itself. "You can't say, 'Thanks for coming in out of the rain, when it's not even raining anymore! You'll look like an idiot!" Another part of my brain said, "You already look like an idiot, hurry up and say something -- anything! The spotlight has been on for five seconds and these people are waiting for you to say something!" In the midst of all this arguing, my inner thoughts should have come up with a complete sentence of something intelligent to say. But aside from all the inner bickering, I could not come up with a thing. I wanted to run for the exit, but I knew we would go live in 12 more minutes and that would end my career.

They say the last thing to go when you lose your memory is your name. I prayed that was true. I opened my mouth and out came, "Hi. My name is Don Corey and I'm from KSHE radio. And I have some albums to give away." I was just about to ask some trivia questions, but I had placed the stack of albums too close to the front of the stage. As soon as they heard "free albums" there was a mad dash to the stage and a brief flurry as the records disappeared. The crowd vanished back into the darkness like a herd of jackals picking over their kill. And there I was. I actually had to ad-lib for the remaining ten minutes, most of which was a blur. I seriously doubt the crowd was warmed up. As for me, I was sweating.

Strange things would happen in my life that was totally unexpected. When I turned 21 years old, some friends wanted to take me out drinking. I didn't drink. Oh, I had tried it a few times, but I just didn't feel the hangover the next day was worth it. My friends insisted, so I decided to humor them just this once.

Prior to this I had gotten an interesting piece of identification. It was a laminated plastic card that was supposed to identify a person of legal drinking age. This was back when the driver's licenses did not bear their owner's picture. This I.D., called a Liquor Control Card, quickly was replaced by a driver's license with a photo on it as a form of identification.

But I'm a "pack rat." I never throw anything away. I kept this card in my wallet even after no one else used them anymore. So my friends and I went to a local bar in the area. As we were carded at the door, I showed my Liquor Control Card while my two buddies showed their driver's licenses.

We got a table and a waitress arrived and asked us what we were drinking. We all ordered some booze and drank a round. The waitress reappeared after a while and we asked how much we owed and she replied, "It's on the house." Great, we thought, and promptly ordered another round. She brought the drinks, we drank them, and again she came back to see if we needed anything else. We asked how much we owed this time, and again she replied, "It's on the house."

Well, we ordered yet another round and after she'd left we started wondering what in the world was going on. "Is this some sort of holiday we're not aware of? " "Is it a special sports promotion or something?" I asked the guys if they'd ever been here before. Neither of them had ever set foot in this bar, they just picked it at random.

Suddenly I said, "Do you think it has anything to do with this?" I showed them the I.D. I had used when I got carded. "Oh my God," one of my friends said, "they think you're a Liquor Control Agent. They probably have under age kids in here drinking and they're 'buying us off' to keep quiet!"

Once again I had wandered into a peculiar situation accidentally. I said, "We'd better get out of here before they figure out we're not with the feds, or we're liable to get dumped in an alley."

The waitress came back one last time and we politely made our exit, after having finished off a good amount of alcohol absolutely free of charge. When I got home, I cut up my Liquor Control Card and never used it again.

Thursday, February 18, 1971 was not only the halfway mark for my stint in the Army Reserves -- three years down, with three more to go -- but also another milestone. I got a raise in pay. Yes, I was now making $4 an hour. By today's standards that seems like nothing, but in 1971 things were looking great! I was

Don Corey

still living at home with my parents, I had purchased a new Pontiac Lemans, I had a smokin' hot girlfriend and life was definitely looking good. When you're young like that, you think it will go on like that forever.

Because I was in the Reserves, I had to go to Summer Camp for two weeks every year and this year was no exception. On Saturday May 8, our company -- the 520th Maintenance Battalion -- left for Camp McCoy in Wisconsin. Being away from KSHE for two weeks was one of the ways I could tell that I really liked my job there. By the middle of the second week, I told my fellow reservists, "Man, I can't wait to get back to work!" Of course, this would cause them to say, "Are you nuts?" No one can believe it when you tell him you love your job so much you can't wait to get back, but that's how I felt.

While we were in Wisconsin, someone had the radio on in the orderly room and there was an announcer doing the news. One of the guys in my platoon came running in and said, "Hey, Don, you have to come hear this guy on the radio. He sounds *just like you!*" I followed him to the orderly room, smiling to myself thinking, "Yeah, I've heard this before." Perhaps you know what I mean. Someone says somebody looks like you, and you see him and think, "Man, they don't look anything like me, are they blind?" So I figured, I'll just listen politely and shake my head and go back to the barracks. But when I heard this guy, it was spooky. He really *did* sound like me -- same cadence, same reflection, it was just uncanny.

At first I thought maybe someone was playing a joke

on me. I thought maybe they'd gotten some of my old radio show tapes and were playing them through a fake radio. But no, this was an actual newscast of things that were going on in the area right at that time period, not anything that could be faked. If this had been all there was to the story, it would have been strange enough. But there was still a clincher to come. Just as we were about to turn off the radio, the newscast ended with the announcer saying, "...that's the news, *Don Corey reporting.*" We all looked at each other and started laughing! One of the guys said, "We have *got* to call the station and tell them!" We grabbed the local phone book, looked up the station's number and called, but the phone rang and rang and no one ever answered.

I was never able to call this guy up and say, "Not only do you sound like me, you've got my name and I'm a fellow disc jockey back in St. Louis." I was so glad to have a room full of guys who witnessed this event. Otherwise, no one would have ever believed it.

One night I'll never forget. I was on the way to work at KSHE and running a little late. Normally I'm very punctual, as anyone has to be when you're on radio. Naturally when you're in a hurry it always seems you get stuck behind a slowpoke on the highway. This was indeed the case this night.

It was some guy in a big old barge of a car -- a Cadillac. He was in the left lane going about 30 miles per hour in a 40-mile-per-hour zone on Watson Road. I'd been behind him for quite a while because there was a vehicle in the right lane, going equally slow. Boxed behind these two fools, I could not get around them.

Don Corey

The term "road rage" hadn't appeared yet, but I think I was probably headed that way. As we approached the bottom of the hill leading toward Crestwood Plaza, the car on the right actually started to go still slower, which allowed me to get into the right lane and come up to the speed limit. As I did this, the Cadillac actually started to increase its speed as well. We were both approaching the bottom of the hill just ahead of the railroad tracks, with my car just slightly behind his. Suddenly, the Cadillac's brake lights came on. He was braking hard! I thought it was because he didn't want to go over the tracks too fast. Since he was braking, and I wasn't, I was about to fly by on his right. I was still a little aggravated at having followed this dimwit for several miles, so I decided to give him a stupid look as I sailed by. As I started past him, I gave him a dumb, sarcastic looking smile, but he had a panicky look on his face as though something horrible was about to happen. In the next second, I found out why.

As I passed his car, still looking left, I saw the oncoming train! The railroad crossing signals had apparently malfunctioned. No lights or bells had warned of the locomotive that was barreling down. He had seen it first and that was why he was panic-stopping. But for me, I was now in its direct path, and it looked huge! I had never seen a train this close up, and it was coming fast! I could hear the train horn now, and I knew it would be only milliseconds before the crash. I snapped my head forward and mashed my foot onto the accelerator. As I floored the car, it lurched forward. At that moment, instead of closing my eyes and waiting for the collision, I looked up at my rear view mirror. In it I saw nothing but boxcars whizzing by. The train must have missed me by mere inches. I actually had to pull over to the side of the road and wait for my stomach.

This was probably as close to death as I had ever been. I had been spared and I had no idea why.

Again in the studio doing my late night show in April 1971, I was happy to be back surrounded in my comfort zone. I had all but forgotten the terrors of being onstage before a live audience. I received a note at the station from Lynn, one of the secretaries. The note said that Concordia Seminary was looking for a disc jockey to give a talk to 36 guys. This seemed a lot less threatening than a crowd of people at a nightclub, so I told Lynn I was up for it.

As the day for my speaking assignment on April 20 grew closer, one of my fellow announcers asked me what I had planned to say. Did I have an outline they wanted to know? No, I was just going to give some brief comments and then just open the floor up for questions. They said, "You have to talk for an hour, don't you? What if no one asks anything?" So I said, "Oh, I don't think that will be a problem. Everyone has questions about music and radio. It'll be fine." I was greeted by that look that says, "Good luck. It's your funeral."

Well the big day came and I arrived at Concordia. The room where I would speak resembled a school classroom with about 40 desks. I stood at the front and watched the guys saunter in and get settled in their seats. At the back of the room was a large wall clock so that I could pace myself to make sure I gave a complete hour. I started at exactly 1:15. By 1:25 I had finished my opening remarks and opened the floor for questions. Not one person raised his hand. Suddenly that panicky feeling was about to raise its ugly head again. Only this time I was ready for it. I looked around the room and said, "You mean to tell me no one has a single question? Not one of you has ever wondered why the commercials on TV sound louder than the rest of the program?" Having said that, I explained why. And hoped this would spark another question. Since it didn't, I simply initiated another question. "Haven't you ever wondered..." and I kept this up until finally a hand shot up. Someone had a question of his own. "Finally!" I thought to myself. I answered that question and now more of the guys got involved. It turned into a lively discussion and we all had a great time! The hour flew by and there were still some hands up when I told them it was time for me to go. It turned out better than I had expected, so much so that I was asked to return again. Rest assured, the next time I came prepared.

In August of 1971 the management told us that any disc jockey who was interested could apply for and receive a Press Card. This card would enable us to "...pass Police lines, except in areas under special security..." Well, I certainly wasn't going to pass up this opportunity. I immediately applied for my card. When it arrived, it went straight into my wallet. I wasn't sure I would ever get the chance to use it. After all, KSHE wasn't exactly known for our "news department." As a matter of fact, we didn't even have one. All we really did was "rip and read" the news as it came across the Teletype machine. It came straight from the Associated Press and we had one news report per hour, usually about a five-minute report, which we called "KSHE news in brief." Nevertheless, I was thrilled at the prospect of having the card. If something newsworthy occurred, I'd be ready.

One night at 2 a.m., I was on the air doing my regular shift, when I heard sirens. I could see flashing lights of emergency vehicles in the distance as they flew east down Watson Road. The record I was playing had about 5 minutes left, so I ran outside and looked down the street. Whatever was happening was at the bottom of the hill, probably less than 3 minutes away by car. I ran back inside and cued up a long track, "Get Ready" by Rare Earth. I started the song and ran out the front door, locking it behind me. I jumped in my car and fired it up, tires squealing as I raced down the driveway and onto Watson Road.

As I approached the bottom of the hill, I saw a small building near the railroad tracks was engulfed in flames. I wasn't sure what this building was, why it was there or what it contained -- but I was going to find out! This was my first chance as a budding news reporter. As far as I knew, KSHE had never done anything like this before. This would be a first.

I jumped out of my car and ran up to a policeman standing near the edge of the roadway. Flashing my press card at him -- in a most professional manner, I thought -- I said to him, over the din of commotion just yards away, "I'm Don Corey from KSHE radio. What's happening here?" The policeman didn't hesitate for a moment with his response. "It's a fire," he said flatly.

Don Corey

I shrugged off this sarcasm and said, "Yes, I can see it's a fire, but is there any indication what might have started the fire?" The policeman said, "Yeah -- somethin' hot."

Man! Talk about having the wind knocked out of your sails. I turned around and headed back to my car. I put away my press card and raced back to the station. A little aggravated at the way I was treated by the policeman, I still wanted this moment to not be a total loss. I called the Associated Press report hotline and told them my story. A short time later the report came over the newswire. It read: "There was a fire of an unknown origin reported in a vacant building on Watson Road in Crestwood, Missouri. No injuries were reported and no other details are available at this time." The byline read "KSHE radio." It was my first and only attempt, as I never used my Press Card again.

Of course, I wasn't the only person who used a Press Card dramatically. Sir Ed, one of the morning DJs. tells the story of our news guy, Richard. He used it to get into a big news conference at the McDonald-Douglas building. The conference featured NASA astronauts -- a very big affair, indeed. Richard's question to the astronauts was, "Do you guys really drink Tang?"

I just loved the late shift at KSHE. One of my favorite things was playing creative music sets. Whenever a thunderstorm would hit, I would immediately start playing songs about rain. The best was "Riders on the Storm," by The Doors; a song simply called, "Rain," by Uriah Heep; "One more rainy day," by Deep Purple; and "Song for a Rainy Tuesday," by Randy Holland. I did this frequently and it became kind of a tradition. One night a friend was playing cards with some of his buddies. It started to thunderstorm and he said, "Go turn on KSHE, they're going to play 'Riders on the Storm.'" One of the guys said, "How do you know that?" "Trust me," he said. They turned it on and sure enough, "Riders on the Storm" was in progress. They all thought he was psychic.

One night was really wild. It started to storm and I was doing my usual rain songs. Looking out the visitor window, I was anxious to see just how bad this storm would get. I was a little frightened. I love thunderstorms, but when you're that close to a 400-foot tall radio tower, it's a little unnerving. The tower was only about two car-lengths away from the studio. They're anchored pretty well, but you never know. The rain was coming faster than I'd ever seen! Suddenly lightning hit the tower. Boom! I nearly jumped out of my skin! The bolt ripped down the tower -- a giant searing white flash that lit up the night as day. Normally you can count seconds between a flash and the thunder, but the flash and the explosion were simultaneous. When I turned around I saw that we were off the air. The record was still playing, but the transmitter was completely shut down. This meant I would have to go to the transmitter room and restart it. I would have to press a big green button – wait a few seconds – and then hopefully everything would come back on. At least that's the way it was supposed to work. I ran to the room and opened the door. I was shocked at what I saw. The rain had come down so rapidly it gushed under the back door and was flooding the transmitter room. Water was everywhere, several inches deep, including directly in front of the transmitter – the place I would be standing when I pressed the button.

I'm not afraid of electricity, but I'm smart enough to have great respect for it. The thought of standing in a puddle of water and attempting to start an electrical device carrying 200,000 watts of power -- let's just say I was going to make a phone call first.

I got the emergency phone number of the Chief Engineer and called him at home. This was about 2:30 a.m. He wasn't exactly thrilled to hear from me. I explained the situation and he was not in the least distressed. "Of course not, what does he care, I'm the one who's going to get fried," I thought to myself. But he assured me. "That transmitter is completely grounded. There's no need to worry." Then he hung up.

As an engineer I'm sure he knew what he was talking about. Nevertheless, I was taking no chances. I placed a large cardboard box directly in front of the transmitter, about arm's length away. I climbed onto the box, and taking the wooden handle of a broomstick, I prepared to press the green start button. I lined up the end of the handle with the center of the button and held my breath as I pressed the broom forward. With a loud "clunk," the relays kicked in as the transmitter sprang to life! I jumped off the box and ran back to the studio. The song that was playing was just finishing up. I was glad to be alive. I'm not superstitious, but after that I never did the rain songs anymore.

I liked taking requests on KSHE. Some of the DJs didn't, because they wanted to pick their own music. I liked it because callers would alert me to songs I hadn't heard before. The Bob Dylan songs I was familiar with, were the ones on AM radio. Like "Rainy Day Women" and "Lay Lady Lay." One night a caller asked me to play, "Desolation Row" by Dylan. It's about 10 minutes long. I don't mind playing long songs -- but Dylan's voice is not what you'd call melodic. After ten minutes, my listeners might well disappear. But the caller said, "It's a great song!" so I played it. The lyrics were phenomenal! It became a personal favorite and I played it frequently.

Another song that was very popular was, "Waiting To Die" by Joe Byrd and the Field Hippies. No, I'm not making this up. The people who called for this request knew it was "way out there," so to ensure I would play it, they would come up with a justification. Some would say, "Hey man, I just got back from Viet Nam, could you play..." Of course, how could I refuse someone who fought for our freedom? Another one was, "Hey, I got some people here, from California ..." because nobody's as hip as somebody from California.

One caller wanted a song. He didn't know the name, or who did it. But he said, "It has the word 'love' in it." Yes, that would certainly narrow it down.

Then there was the night a guy called to request, "For What It's Worth" by Buffalo Springfield. This song got played frequently on AM radio. At KSHE we tried to steer clear of anything being played to death elsewhere. But this song is a classic, so I said, "Sure I'll play that." I found the album and cued it up. A moment later the request line blinked again, so I answered. The caller said, "Will you play, 'For What It's Worth' by Buffalo Springfield?" I said, "Didn't you just call?" The guy said, "No way, man -- that must have been somebody else." I smiled and said, "Yeah, no problem, I'll get it on for you." The record that was playing had about a minute left. The request line blinked again. I answered and the caller – it was the same guy – disguised his voice and said, "Can you play 'For What It's Worth' by Buffalo Springfield?" I could not believe it. I said, "Listen, I know this is you again, you've called me three times now about the same song. I already told you I'd play it, and I will. But if you call one more time I'm going to warp it over a hot light bulb and then nobody's going to play it!" The guy said, "O.K. man." I hung up the phone. I watched to see if the request line would blink again. "If this guy calls once more I am *not* going to play this song." A minute went by. No call. I guess he got the hint. I keyed the microphone and said, "Now, by request, here's Buffalo Springfield." I started the song and turned off the mike.

The request line blinked again. When I answered, the caller said, "Thanks for playing my song a**hole!" and hung up. Unbelievable! I quickly cued up another song. I keyed the mike and said, "Due to circumstances beyond our control, this song will not be played at this time." I faded out the Buffalo Springfield song and turned up the other one. The request line blinked again. I knew who it was. I did not answer.

A peculiar thing happened one night after KSHE was "off the air." Back then the station would leave the air once a week to perform equipment tests. This particular night we were scheduled to take the station down at 3 a.m. At 2:59, I made the announcement that we would be leaving the air to perform equipment tests, and that KSHE would resume its regular broadcasting at 6 a.m. I turned off the microphone as the Chief Engineer headed for the transmitter room.

A tone generator was plugged into the control board. My task was to input tones at certain frequencies and volume levels as directed by the engineer. We waited about 10 or 15 minutes until we were sure everyone had tuned away. The engineer said, "Give me 1,000 cycles." I turned the dial and pressed the "send" key. A 1,000-cycle tone is the high-pitched sound you hear during "Emergency Broadcast" tests. It's very jarring and not very pleasant to the ears. This continued for about 30 seconds until he got the reading he was looking for. Then he said, "Now give me 440 cycles." This was a moderate tone, the equivalent of "middle C" on a piano, much easier on the ear. After 45 seconds of this tone, he asked for "60 cycles." This is a very low sound, like the rumbling of distant thunder.

After about 10 minutes of these varied tones, I noticed the request line was blinking. I alerted the engineer and he told me to answer it. Perhaps it was important. I grabbed the phone and said, "KSHE." The caller said, "Uh, can you play me a request?" I hesitated for a moment; I said, "We're not playing requests right now, we're doing equipment tests." The guy said, "Oh, wow man...is *that* what that is? I thought it was some weird song. I was wondering why there wasn't any drums or anything."

Don Corey

Yeah. That might have been a clue. I told him to tune back in after 6 a.m. and we'd be glad to play a song for him. What I really wanted to say was, "Be careful when you hang up the phone. I wouldn't want you to knock over your bong water."

Another fun thing about the midnight shift was that I got to play the "long songs." I did this for two good reasons. First, there were a lot of great songs out there the other stations weren't playing. I considered it my sworn duty to make sure these got heard: "Get Ready" by Rare Earth; the long version of "By the time I get to Phoenix" by Isaac Hayes; "The Monster" by Steppenwolf; and, of course, the long version of "In-A-Gadda-Da-Vida" by Iron Butterfly. One of my personal favorites was "Salisbury" by Uriah Heep. But the granddaddy of all was the "Who Do You Love Suite" by Quicksilver Messenger Service. This was the longest track in the studio. Taking up a whole album side, it was some 25 minutes and 22 seconds long. Which brings me to reason number two. It gave me more time to talk to girls on the phone. Yes, I'm sorry, I was a terrible flirt.

Another long song I played only occasionally was "Alice's Restaurant Massacree" by Arlo Guthrie. I didn't play it a lot. Not because it was 18 minutes long. It was because it was really more of a story than a song. It's pure genius, but not something you can play often without alienating listeners. So I would simply let the listeners decide.

I'd announce, "I'm thinking about playing, 'Alice's Restaurant.' If you'd like to hear it, call in now and vote 'yes.' If you'd rather not hear it, call in and vote,

'No.' The lines will be open for voting only, for the next five minutes." At the end of five minutes, I'd tally the votes. The "yes" vote was usually in the majority. I'd say, "The 'Ayes' have it. If you voted to *not* hear the song, please come back in 18 and a half minutes from now, and I'll be happy to play something *you'd* like to hear." This plan seemed to be equitable to everyone.

Another night something odd occurred. It was a beautiful summer evening; the temperature was an almost perfect 70 degrees. I had the visitor window open and tilted at the maximum angle enjoying the cool summer breeze. I went to the transmitter room to take the required readings. The building was locked and I was alone. A 12 minute song was playing and it was about 3 a.m. Suddenly I heard a horrible sound coming from the monitor speakers. It was a loud, "ZZZZZZZZZZZ" followed by a sound like a concrete truck skidding upside down on a gravel road. I ran back to the control room to see what had happened. The tone arm had skidded all the way across the album and was riding atop the paper label of the album. What in the world could have caused this calamity? I immediately grabbed up the tone arm, keyed the microphone and said, "Well, that was interesting."

Then I saw it. A June bug had flown in the window and landed right on the spinning record. There he was, on his back with his legs kicking in the air. I told the listeners what had occurred and re-started the record. All six of the request lines lit up. Everybody wanted to know, "if that really happened." I said, "Who would make up a story like that?" One caller said, "That was the most horrible thing I ever heard! I almost drove off the road! Why did it go on for so long?" I explained that I got there as fast as I could. I had to run down a hallway and make three sharp turns. We all had a good laugh about it. I kept the June bug in a jar to show the other DJs, just in case they thought I made up the whole story. I guess you could say this was simply a case of a "June bug going on record."

The KSHE visitor window was a full size glass allowing visitors to see into the control room while the live broadcast was going on. At waist level was a tilt-in window with a locking lever. I kept this window open when the weather was nice, which sometimes created problems. Occasionally people outside would yell in when they knew the microphone was on. It was the audio version of "streaking" I supposed. Not as exciting or fulfilling, but they seemed to like it.

One night a guy stopped by about three in the morning to buy concert tickets. He asked how much they cost. I told him, "Four dollars apiece." He said, "How much for two?" At first I thought he was talking about a quantity discount. Then I realized it was because he was stoned and couldn't add four and four! He bought the tickets and I gave him his change. He lifted a paper bag, put it to his face and breathed into it. I think he was sniffing glue. He held the bag in my direction and said, "Hey dude, you want some?" I told him, "No thanks." To myself I thought, "No, I can see what it's done to you. I want to live a long, healthy life, that includes being able to add four and four." Then he wanted to "hang around and talk." I thought, "What in the world would we talk about? The guy can't add two simple numbers together." I wanted to think of a way to make leave without hurting his feelings, assuming he still had any. So I replied, "Uh, I don't think that'd be a good idea. The Crestwood Police drive by here frequently to make sure I'm o.k." This got his immediate attention. Even in his drug-induced stupor, the word police managed to cut through. He thanked me and left.

There really was a nice policeman named Rick who would stop by occasionally. He liked country music. Since KSHE did not play country music, I would salvage the albums and give them to him. One night he did something funny. During my shift I usually kept the overhead lights off, and just a small table lamp on. This gave off just enough light for me to see the controls. It helped me to create a mood to enhance my choice of music.

Knowing this, Rick quietly drove his squad car up to the window. He got as close to the building as his front bumper would allow. I did not hear the crunching of his tires on the gravel, because I had my headphones on. Then he turned on his spotlight and shined it through the window. The room lit up like an atomic bomb went off. I jumped out of my chair thinking, "The mother ship must have landed!" When I saw him standing outside his patrol car and laughing, I said, "That's real cute, Rick. One more stunt like that and it's no more country music for you!"

One night I made the mistake of mentioning that I was hungry. Within minutes people were driving up to the window with food of all kinds. They brought burgers and fries, pizza -- somebody even brought an apple pie! I had to go back on the air and say, "Thanks so much to all of you but please, don't bring any more food!"

Almost every night there was a crowd at the window and lots of phone calls. People called to request a song, or maybe they were bored or lonely. But one night there were no visitors. The phone hadn't rung for an hour. When the record faded out I said, "Am I just sitting here talking to myself? Is anybody out there?" The phone lines lit up. As soon as I answered, the caller said, "We're out here, man -- we're just digging the music! You're doing great, keep it up." Other callers related the same message. This taught me a valuable lesson. Sometimes when the phone isn't ringing, it's because you're doing it right.

One of the things radio stations must do to keep their license is to run public service announcements, also known as PSA's. The spots that KSHE ran were quite interesting. In the 70's there was a big problem with young kids taking "speed." Many deaths were attributed to this form of drug abuse. In light of this fact, KSHE chose to run PSA's to try to discourage drug use. Artists in the record industry recorded most of these announcements. There was Jefferson Airplane, The Grateful Dead, and Grand Funk Railroad to name just a few. My favorite was by Frank Zappa. He did edicts about not using "speed." One of them went like this: "This is Frank Zappa of the Mothers of Invention. You're going to die from using 'speed.' You like that? You're going to die from using it. Put 'speed' down. Do it now. Be a good sport."

One morning, at 5:00, I played that spot. Suddenly the

request line blinked. I picked up the phone and a girl on the other end was frantic. She said she always listened to my show on her alarm clock radio. She would set it so that it would turn off after an hour, and then it would come back on at 5 a.m. to wake her with music instead of a blaring alarm.

When her clock came on this morning, instead of music, she heard a male voice say, "You're going to die." She bolted straight up in her bed thinking there was a stranger in the room, about to do her bodily harm. When she realized it was just the radio, she said, "I just *had* to call and tell you about it!" We both got a big laugh about the strange way it happened.

It did strike me as ironic that the guys in rock bands were telling everyone not to do drugs. It seemed to me the majority of them were doing it themselves. I guess it was a case of "Don't do the drugs -- leave them for us." As for myself, I didn't do recreational drugs. I was bizarre enough with just my normal personality. Besides, I'm not sure I'd take any drug advice from Jerry Garcia.

Around this time there was a rumor going around that Paul McCartney was dead. People were constantly calling in on the request line asking about it. They cited all kinds of clues found on their albums. People were actually playing records backwards in search of more clues. Many of them completely ruined the vinyl by doing this. They didn't know you have to have a conical stylus to back-cue. If the stylus is elliptical, it destroys the record and usually the stylus as well.

I personally thought the whole thing was ridiculous.

Don Corey

After several of these crazy calls one night, I opened the microphone and said, "This thing that's going around about Paul McCartney being dead -- it's just a stupid rumor. It's a hoax. There's absolutely no truth to it. " After I finished this statement, the phone line rang. I picked it up and the caller said, "What's that about Paul McCartney being dead?"

Radio stations love to be "first." Not only radio, but television and newspapers too. They'll say things like, "You heard it first on XYZ" or "This is follow up on a story you heard first on XYZ." In radio this was called an "exclusive."

Although KSHE billed itself as a "Progressive Rock" and even "Underground" station, it was not exempt from this rush to be first. A new album by John Lennon had just come out in December of 1970. Shelly, the station manager came running into the studio. "We've got the new Lennon album," he said, "no one else has it. It's an exclusive!" He was speaking to the morning DJ who came on after my show. He wanted him to hurry, so KSHE would be the first to play it. The DJ asked, "Do you want me to audition a cut?" (Audition means to play a song on the cue speaker before taking it to the air.) Shelly shook his head and said, "No. Just pick a cut and get it on the air." He handed him the album and the DJ picked a selection at random. He introduced it as a song from "the new John Lennon album" and started the song.

Of all the songs he could have picked, he chose "Working Class Hero." Here's where the fun begins. The song is quiet, almost Dylan-like, with a single acoustic guitar and Lennon's vocal. Very subdued, down tempo, a nice song really. Until a minute and two seconds in -- along comes the "F word." The word is not hidden by loud guitar licks or crashing drums. It's right out there -- could not miss it if you tried. Shelly comes running back to the studio and says, "Did I hear what I think I heard?" The DJ says, "Yeah." Shelly says, "Maybe it won't get any worse." No such luck. At the two minute and twenty second mark, along comes the "F word" again. Just as clear as the first time. Now the phones are going crazy. Guys are calling in saying, "Man, what a great song! When are you going to play it again?" This is going to be a problem. Neither Shelly nor the DJ had any idea what was on that track when they played it. Now that they know, however, it's a whole different scenario.

Several days later, Shelly took me to the side and said, "We've had a lot of requests for 'Working Class Hero' but we can't play it. Take it into the production room and bleep out the bad words." I said, "Should I edit a tone in place of the word?" He said, "That'd be too obvious, just leave a blank space so it won't call attention to it." I cut the two offending words out as gingerly as I could and we put it on tape and started playing the new version. Now the listeners called in saying, "I can't believe you guys are censoring songs! What ever happened to the old KSHE?" Sometimes you just can't win no matter what you do. We finally ended up not playing the song at all.

The way the KSHE studio was arranged, two Gates turntables were to the DJs left, the albums were on the right and the control board straight ahead. The start switches were located on the turntables themselves, so the closest one was no problem at all.

Don Corey

The other was a pretty far reach. The DJs asked the management if we could get remote start switches installed. It was decided that the best time to do it would be the midnight shift, because there's fewer commercials and not a lot of people running around.

The big night came and the engineer came in around two in the morning. He set down his toolbox and asked me, "Can you do without both turntables for about an hour?" I said, "Not unless you want me to sing." He didn't find this particularly amusing so I immediately jumped in with a suggestion. "I could record some songs onto tape and we could play those." He agreed that would work just fine. I said, "Are you sure it'll only take an hour?" He assured me that an hour would be all that was necessary.

I started a long song on the air, and ran to the production room. I began to record songs onto tape cartridges, running back and forth between studios to make sure the records hadn't run out. An hour and ten minutes later I had a stack of tape carts with an hour and ten minutes worth of music. The extra ten minutes would be a safeguard in case the engineer miscalculated. I gave the station I.D. and started the first tape. He unplugged both of the turntables and set about the task of installing the remote switches. As I played each tape I watched intently to see how the work was progressing. Almost an hour had passed and I was almost down to my emergency 10 minutes worth of tapes. "Almost ready?" I asked "Not yet, pretty soon" came his reply.

Now I was getting nervous. I ran to the production room and started to record another song to tape. It was more difficult now, because I no longer had the luxury of a long song on album. If I had a six-minute song on the air, I could only record a 5-minute song on tape. Then I'd run back to the studio before the six-minute song ran out. With less than a minute leeway, each subsequent song got a little closer to the run-out mark. I was running back and forth like a wild man. I thought I would lose my mind. Finally, he told me the switches were ready to go. He applied the power to the turntables and left the room to clean up the mess.

As he headed down the hall, I placed an album on the turntable and pushed the toggle switch marked turntable one. It did not come on. Turntable two, however, started right up. The switches were reversed. I thought for a moment -- maybe I shouldn't tell him. After all, it would be a simple matter to just press turntable two when I wanted turntable one. By the time he returned, I had reluctantly decided. "Well, how're they working?" "Uh- they're just fine," I replied, "it's just that -- when you push number one -- number two starts up." He looked at me. Then looked at the switches. And he began to curse. It's a good thing my microphone wasn't on. He muttered several more swear words as he left the room. As he went down the hall I heard him say, "I *knew* I should have gone on vacation!" Still ranting as he went into the transmitter room, I saw things flying by as he hurled them. I began to wish I hadn't mentioned this minor flaw.

Eventually he cooled down and came back. He told me to change the labels on the two switches and he would work on it again later. I said I'd be happy to do

Don Corey

that. He left, locking the door behind him. I turned the studio lights down low and put on the Moody Blues. I took some calls from my listeners -- and once again the world was all right.

KSHE 1969

Don Corey

I always liked to stretch the listener's imagination on my show. I figured hey, if you can't do it on the midnight shift, where's it going to happen? One night I decided to try something a little different, just for fun. We had a song in the studio called, "Don't Bogart that joint" by Fraternity of Man. In the song one of the verses has the word "roll" in it. The vocalist drags the word out for about four seconds. I decided to play a little trick on my listeners. A portion of the late night audience tended to be -- how could I put this delicately -- feeling no pain, very relaxed. Yes, and it was in this light I decided what I had to do. I took the album into the production room and copied it onto a reel of tape. I then carefully edited the tape so that the word "roll" increased from a mere four seconds to a full 30 seconds. I took the song into the studio. I didn't mention the fact that it was altered. I simply played the song.

When it got to the edited part -- "Roooooooooooooooool" -- it seemed to go on even longer than 30 seconds. It seemed like it would never end. It almost took on the feeling of the long tone during the E.B.S. test. Finally the word ended and the song continued. The way it was edited, it didn't sound like a "skipping" record, it was just a smooth continuance. The song wasn't even finished yet when the request lines started blinking like crazy. When I answered, the guy said, "Hey, was there like, something wrong with that song? It seemed like it was stuck or something." I said, "No man, you must be stoned or something." I answered the next call. "K-SHE." "Hey, was there something weird about that last song?" "No dude, you sure you're not 'on something'?" I answered these calls for several minutes until the song ran out. I went on the air and said," That was the Fraternity of Man with, 'Don't Bogart that joint' and yes, I have a confession to make. I extended the word 'roll.' It wasn't your imagination. Just thought you might enjoy it." Now the phone lines really went nuts. Callers were saying, "Man, you freaked me out! That was amazing! Can you do that again tomorrow night? I want some friends of mine to hear it." I had to tell them no, it was just a one shot deal.

Usually I would come up with these crazy ideas all on my own. One night something occurred that wasn't my idea. There was a station on the FM dial called KDNA. The station was located in Gaslight Square and was truly an "underground" station. They played some of the strangest things you would ever hear on the radio. It was listener supported and not many people even knew it was out there. And boy, was it *out there*. They would allow people to come in off the street and DJ. Occasionally you'd tune in and a record had 'run out' and there was just a click-click-click sound of the stylus riding around in an empty groove.

This particular night I answered the request line and a guy named Alan was on the air at KDNA. He asked if I'd like to participate in a little "experiment." I asked what he had in mind. He said that he had the DJ from KADI on the other line. The idea was to come up with a song that all three of us had and then to play them simultaneously on all three stations. It sounded like great idea. We spent the next few minutes trying to find a song all three of us had. At last we came up with, "Fresh Air" by Quicksilver Messenger Service. All

Don Corey

three of us cued the record and waited for Alan to give the signal. We all started the song at the same exact moment. I said goodbye to Alan and the KADI guy. I hung up the phone and ran out to my car radio. Sure enough, all across the dial the same song was playing at exactly the same time. I ran back to the studio and the calls were already starting to come in. "Did you know you're playing the exact same song that KADI and KDNA are playing?" "Really, " I said, "what a colossal coincidence!"

If the management had found out I might have been in trouble. In radio you're not supposed to talk to the 'competition.' I still think it was a fun thing to do.

Alan later went to San Francisco. KDNA disappeared from the airwaves. KADI changed call letters and owners several times.

FOURTEEN

It was April of 1973. KSHE had a clipboard in the studio that we could use to make comments. It was like a "suggestion box" without the box. There would be remarks like:

"The new B.B. King album has a scratch and should be replaced."

"People are asking about the new '*White Album*' by the Beatles."

"Some listeners are complaining because we're running beer commercials."

Richard Fendell was doing the news for KSHE. He had a very unique way of doing this. These were recorded on tape and consisted of an introductory piece of music. It was a peppy up-tempo song called, "One Fine Morning" by a group called Lighthouse.

Richard then hand picked an appropriate musical selection to introduce each news story. If the article dealt with the surgeon general's warning about tobacco use, he would play, "It's nature's way to telling you something's wrong" by a group named Spirit. He did this with each story and then finished with "Layla," by Derek and the Dominos.

This was sheer genius. To take a boring newscast and put an intellectual spin on it and make it entertaining -- that was pure gold. The listeners thought so too. People would call in to ask when the news was scheduled to run again so they could tell their friends when to tune in.

Then Richard was suddenly let go. I did not know why, but I knew the result. The DJs were commissioned to take over the job that Richard had done so well. Sadly, the DJs did *not* do so well. Instead of choosing songs that fit the stories, they just slapped on any song and spoke the news over it. That was lame, but at least had a smidgen of variety. Other DJs would just play one instrumental song and simply turn the volume up and down between stories. There was no comparison between Richard's newscast and these other feeble attempts.

After a short time, management decided this wasn't working and they did away with the music and news combo entirely. We went back to reading the news live. To me it was a poor turn of events and I decided to say so. I wrote a note to stick on the suggestion clipboard. It read: "I think the loss of Richard Fendell, coupled with the policy of reading news live, is a step in the wrong direction." I signed my name, put the note on the clipboard and hung it back on the wall.

Are You Talking To Me?

A week passed and nothing was said about the note. Monday, March 12th, I was called to the station manager's office. He shut the door and sat behind his desk. He threw the note down and said, "Did you write that?" I said, "Of course I did, I signed my name to it." He said, "I don't know what would prompt you to write something like that." I said, "I think everybody here feels that way, I was the only one to put it in writing." He said, "I don't think you know your fellow employees very well. You're terminated at this time." I felt like I'd been punched in the gut. My heart was pounding. I could not believe I was being fired for voicing an opinion. I said, "Just like that? After four and a half years?" He said, "Yeah, just like that." I stood up and said, "Thanks for the memories," and I walked out.

I got in my car to drive home. Everything seemed unreal. I felt empty inside. That old saying came into my head, "When God closes a door, He opens up another one." That's fine, but did He have to slam this one so hard?

This was not just a lost job. This was like the death of a friend. I went through the stages. Denial, anger -- but I was a very long way from acceptance.

I loved radio but now I felt betrayed. I did not have a back door. I had planned on staying in radio until I dropped dead at the mike in my old age. Now I didn't know what I would do. With little education, radio may have been fulfilling, but it didn't do much for my resume. I looked for work and found none. Thankfully I was still in the Army Reserves so I had some income. They say when you "fall off the horse, you should get right back on." In November I got a job on KADI 96 FM. On the air from 1 to 6 in the morning, it just didn't feel the same. KSHE was like family to me. This felt like a corporation. I thought, well, it's radio, I'll get used to it.

I had only been there a few months. I was getting ready to drive to work. It had snowed that night and the roads were treacherous. Slipping and sliding, I managed to get to the station without skidding off the road. As I walked in, Rich Dalton was on the air. I noticed he had a guy in the studio with him. This was strange because we weren't allowed visitors in the studio after hours. It wasn't like Rich to break the rules. I said to him, "Sneaking in a visitor, huh?" He looked at me sadly and said, "No man, that's your replacement. You don't work here anymore." I just stared at him in disbelief. Trying to grasp if he was playing some sort of cruel joke. "I'm sorry, man. I'm sorry you had to hear it from me," Rich said. I said, "Why didn't they call me at home and tell me before I drove here in the snow?" Rich just shook his head and said, "You'll have to call 'P.E.P ' in the morning." (P.E.P. stood for Peter E. Parisi. He was the program director.) I turned around and left the station. Driving home, I listened to this new guy doing what should have been my show. I was angry and hurt again. Not like before -- this was totally different -- but it still hurt.

The next morning I called "P.E.P." and asked why I'd been let go. He said, "You didn't do anything wrong, but Richard didn't like your show." That sounded fishy to me so I immediately hung up and called back to speak to Richard, the station manager. When Richard came on the line, I asked him why I was let go. He said, "You didn't do anything wrong, but P.E.P. didn't like your show." So there it was. There was no reason whatsoever for my being fired. Apparently when I called they didn't have time to get their story straight.

Now I was really miffed. First KSHE, for offering an opinion and now fired for no reason? What kind of craziness is this? I felt totally betrayed by the profession to which I had given my heart. Not my heart and soul. No, I saved my soul for God alone. Good thing.

The dream I had been chasing did not turn out as I had hoped, but I gave it another try. I got a job at KIRL radio, 1460 AM, as a news director. I also did a regular DJ shift on weekends. At the same time I landed a part time gig at a nightclub called "The Scenery Beanery." I helped the owner of the club set up a discotheque. I donated my own equipment and played records there nightly. I would leave the Beanery about Midnight and had to be at KIRL by 6 a.m. Many nights I slept on the couch in the front office at KIRL before doing the news. I was making good money, but the double shifts were taking their toll. I had to decide. Which to quit? The nightclub? The station? Radio was no longer my best friend, so I gave my notice and left KIRL. Two weeks later the Beanery went out of business. Out on the street again. I sat down and wrote these words:

I've an appointment for quarter past nine. Tell the doctor I got here on time.
I don't mind the wait, but I've been here since eight.
I've read the magazines 22 times.
I've just got a case of a broken heart. My world is

Don Corey

slowly coming apart.
If you think there's room, put me back in the womb.
I'd like to make a new start.
I've got my opinion about why I'm here. If you ask
me, I'll talk in your ear.
I'm slightly deranged, and I need to be changed. I've
got to find me another career.

Later these words were put to music with the help of
a friend named Roger. I didn't go see a psychiatrist.
Maybe I should have, I don't know. But after I wrote it
down, I felt better. I went through a period of
voracious writing, some of which was inspirational –
some only fit for the ashcan. But I discovered how
cathartic it was to write. I loved it. Perhaps even more
than radio. In radio I played other people's words.
When writing, the words were mine to choose. I could
speak my heart and not worry about getting fired.

It's been said, "When life hands you lemons, make
lemonade." I had always interpreted this to mean,
"Avoid the lemons." It has taken a long time to learn
to not run away, but learn what the lemon is trying to
tell me. I've forgiven the dream that went sour. I've
acknowledged my gratitude for all the things I've
done that I might have missed, had radio not kicked
me to the curb.

FIFTEEN

No longer a disc jockey, I still had to earn a living. I went through a dizzying assortment of jobs including manager of a pizza parlor, cashier at a quick shop, and bartender/disco announcer for The Fifth House tavern in downtown St. Louis. None of these positions were what I would call a career. Not by a long shot. Then I stumbled upon an opportunity that would be another bit of serendipity. I applied for a position as an audio salesman at a department store in Clayton. At the corner of Hanley and Forsyth, it was Anchor Distributors. I had never sold anything, but I hoped those years of entrepreneurial spirit might help.

The man who interviewed me was David Seifert. He asked some questions about my background. I already knew about electronic equipment. I'd been fooling around with it since I was ten. The question was, could I actually sell the stuff? At the end of the

Don Corey

interview David looked at me and said, "I think you'll make an excellent salesman." He hired me.

David told me there were two types of people I would be helping with their sound systems. One would be an average person, just looking for great sound. He doesn't know much about specifications. He doesn't care. He just wants great sound. The other type is the "tech-head" who is into decibels, harmonics, watts and frequency response. David said to make sure I didn't confuse the two. If I mentioned a technical term, and the customer got a blank look -- to stop and explain the term before continuing. Otherwise I might lose the person, and the sale.

One of my first customers was a man who needed speakers for his stereo. He seemed knowledgeable about technical terms and everything was clicking. I had just mentioned "frequency response," when he suddenly got that puzzled look that David had warned me about. I stopped and said, "Do you know what 'frequency response' means?" He said, "Sure." So I said, "Oh. You got a funny look as though I'd lost you." He replied, "It's not that. It's your voice. I could swear you sound familiar and I don't know why." I said, "Well, I used to be on the radio. Maybe you heard my show." His face brightened and he said, "Were you on midnights? On KSHE?" I nodded and he said excitedly, "I used to listen to you all the time! You always played the Moody Blues and Bob Dylan!" This was a real treat. He was excited because he got to meet the guy who played his favorite music. I got to meet a fan face-to-face. I think I was more excited than he was.

Are You Talking To Me?

People tend to rise to the level that is expected of them. I wanted to prove Mr. Seifert's assessment of me was correct. I determined that I would be that excellent salesman. He gave me several books to study and I zealously gobbled up every fact. I quickly found there was much more than meets the eye -- or ear -- when it comes to audio.

I also found there was more to selling than I imagined. I threw myself into the assignment with abandon, yet it was not as easy as I thought it would be. I mistakenly assumed that if I could talk to people, and had enough knowledge of the product, the sale should be a piece of cake. There would be no cake for me. My technique, if you can call it that, was to make the prospect my friend. Then I would describe the benefits of the equipment, rattling on and on about features. Then I'd make my closing statement and wait to hear, "I'll take it." Those words were rarely heard in my first attempts. Oh, I made plenty of friends, but I did not make plenty of sales. Thankfully I was on an hourly rate and not commission or I would have starved.

Slowly, painfully, I found out what was wrong. The key to sales, I discovered, was to listen more than speak. As a former DJ this was a hard lesson. I had to ask questions and pay close attention to the answers. Give options. Be honest. The hardest part to learn was "the close." Asking for the sale seemed so -- pushy. It didn't feel comfortable. But I had to decide. Do I want to be comfortable, or do I want to succeed? Do I want to make friends, or make money?

This was a big step. I did not want to be overly aggressive – still, I wanted to prove to David that he hadn't made a mistake by believing in me. The first time I asked for the sale, I held my breath and waited for the customer to agree. Seconds ticked by. The silence was deafening. I wanted to say, "Well, if you want to just think about it, I could give you my business card," but I held my tongue and waited. Finally, the customer said, "Let's go ahead and write it up." I was so thrilled I almost hugged him! I knew this was a career I could live with. I also thought it a bit ironic. I had come full circle. I started selling over a speaker system in a department store, now I was selling to people one-on-one. My thoughts returned to the question I had asked myself. Do I want to make friends or make money? The answer to that question was – I could do both! I befriended my customers by being honest and making sure they got the best value for their money. They in turn told people they knew and soon I had more customers, more friends – and more money!

I succeeded in my goal of making David proud. A short time later I was promoted to Audio Room Manager. I came full circle again when I got the chance to write commercials that aired on the radio. I was the "Anchor Answer Man." I wrote and produced the spots myself. Here's one of my favorites: "Anchor Distributors Audio Showrooms presents the Anchor Answer Man. Today's question comes from Dave Roberts of Columbia, Missouri. He wants to know which record cleaner is the best. Well, Dave, the best thing to really clean records is battery acid and a steel brush. This will usually clean the label right off, along with the grooves and the music. However, if you want clean records that still play, you'll want to pick up the Discwasher. "

I also had a column in our newsletter called "The Audio Corner." I had the privilege of working with really great people. There was Gary "the Lip" Lipkin, Ray Lorenz, Charles Kennedy and David Young. Everything was great. One day at our usual morning meeting, the management said Anchor Distributors was closing. We asked, "For a week? A month?" "Permanently," they replied. We were all in shock. None of us saw this coming. They later reopened as Dolgins but by then I had already moved on. David Young went on to start his own company, "The Sound Room." I was upset at Anchor's closing, but I now had something that no one could take away. Something I could take with me to my next position and use as I saw fit. I had a marketable skill. I could sell. It didn't matter what. As long as I believed in it and people needed it, I would never have to be out of a job again.

Selling stereo equipment was fun. It seemed I had finally found my niche. But life was about to throw me another curve, in fact several curves. I had gone from Anchor to Best Sound Company to Best Buy. I was with Silo Superstores, but shortly after my boss Rick Meyers promoted me to Assistant manager, the store closed. I subsequently worked for Video Concepts but just as I was about to be promoted to manager, the chain went out of business. At that point I was wondering if maybe God is trying to tell me something.

I could not find another audio sales position. The store I tried next said they had no need for audio salespeople at all. They did, however, need an appliance salesperson. I took the job. You'd think selling appliances would be an easy step from selling electronics. They're not nearly as complicated, and people need them. It's not just a whim. When your refrigerator fails, you have to have another. It should have been a piece of cake. Once more, there would be no cake for me.

Nothing I had done or witnessed until now had prepared me for the craziness I would discover when working with the public at large. I had heard about the "mob mentality" but I had no idea this extended to retail shoppers. Until now I had found most folks friendly and congenial. But these people were a different breed. The fangs would come out -- and the horns.

Case in point: I approached a man and a woman who were looking at dishwashers. I said, "Hi there." The man spoke first. "Hi." The woman said nothing. I said, "Looking at dishwashers today?" The man answered, "You could say that." The woman still said nothing. I'm wondering if she's mute. I ask the man, "How old is your current dishwasher?" He replies, "How high is up?" I'm not sure how I'm going to respond to this, when suddenly the woman says, "Why are you asking him all the questions? What the hell am I here for?" I said, "Well, he was doing all the talking, " She snapped, "He always does that!" So I turned toward the woman and said, "What do *you* want to accomplish today?" The woman snarled, "I don't know *what* I want. Just give me a price range." So I said, "All right. The least expensive is, " The woman cut me off mid sentence -- "I don't want the least expensive." "That's fine," I said, "It's just that you asked for a price *range*, so I was explaining that the least expensive was," The woman cut me off again *shouting*, "I DON'T WANT THE LEAST EXPENSIVE!"

I glanced at the man and he had a look on his face that said, "Just be glad you're not married to her." I said to them, "Will you excuse me for a moment?"

I quickly ran to my fellow salesperson, Carolyn. "I think we have a personality clash going on in the dishwasher area. These folks are openly hostile and I don't know why. Perhaps you would have better luck." Carolyn went there and they treated her like the Queen had just arrived. At first I didn't understand. I found out later, some people just don't like a certain type to wait on them.

The following day I attempted to greet a woman looking at a clothes washer. I hadn't opened my mouth when she held up her hand like a traffic cop stopping a car. "I don't want a man to help me," she said. No mistaking this meaning. I simply nodded and went off to find Carolyn. The woman had probably experienced a bad male salesperson recently. I didn't take it personally, although I did think it was an odd sort of prejudice. But that door swings both ways. There were instances in which a man didn't want a woman to help him. Carolyn would come and get me. It worked out pretty well. Almost like good cop/ bad cop, except without the rubber hose and the handcuffs.

There were times when the cute little "ad-libs" that served me so well in the radio business -- did not work so well on the sales floor. One occurred when a customer had just entered the store. An over-zealous sales person immediately greeted him. The customer said, "I don't like to be greeted as soon as I come in the door." I replied, "There's where you made your mistake. You should have come in through the window." I thought this ad-lib was brilliantly executed. After all, there was the irony. There were no windows in the store. My intent was to disarm the tension. Unfortunately it had the opposite effect. The customer said, "Oh, you're a funny man, I'll never shop here again," and he turned and left.

Another time I approached a woman who was looking at a dishwasher. Before I could speak she said, "Someone told me you could put me in a dishwasher for a hundred and fifty dollars." I deadpanned, "I don't think you'll fit." I was greeted by a blank stare and silence. "It's a joke," I said. "Oh," the woman replied and started rattling off a barrage of questions.

The worst episode was the night a man and a woman came in looking for an inexpensive clothes washer. As I greeted them, the man said, "I want you to show us your cheapest washer." I led him to our advertised special. Clearly marked "Sale," it was $129.00. He looked at it with distain and said, "Humph. I can get one down the street for $110.00." I looked at him and said, "What are you going to get for $110? A rock and a bowl of water?" I said this in jest, but the customer did not find it the least bit amusing. "Come on dear, " he said to his wife, "let's get out of here."

The two of them headed for the front door. I ran frantically behind them saying, "It was a joke! I meant no disrespect. It was just a joke!" They didn't look back -- they just kept on going. I had visions of being fired so I went to the store manager and explained what happened. He laughed and told me not to worry about it. I told him I'd hate to get fired because somebody didn't have a sense of humor. He said it probably wasn't the joke at all. The man might have been angry that I unwittingly called his bluff. Nowhere in town could he have gotten a new washer that cheap. He was trying to get us to drop the price. I wasn't sure if that was true. I was just glad I wasn't getting canned over another of my one-liners.

Another time I was helping a young boy pick out his first clothes washer. He asked to use the store phone. He picked it up, dialed a number and said, "Hey mom, I'm down here looking at washers. If I start washing my underwear, those sores might heal up." Nearby customers overheard this remark and looked at me. I just shrugged. No way I could top that line.

One day I tried to help a lady decide which refrigerator she wanted. After a half hour agonizing over which was the best, she told me she wanted me to take the door off the refrigerator so she could take it home. She wanted to make sure the almond color matched her stove. I explained that although we could not do that, I would be happy to supply her with a small sample of the almond color that she could take with her. I also explained that after delivery and set up, if she did not like how it looked for *any reason*, we would return it to the store and give her a complete refund. She did not care for either of these ideas, and insisted that I remove the door so she could be on her way. I said, "We really can't do that." She said, "I guess you don't want the sale very much." I replied, "Not if that's what it takes, no." She left.

I was learning the hard way -- the way I learned most everything in life -- that my quick tongue wasn't always a good thing. As a DJ this ability served me well but now I found myself in situations that would have been better suited to thoughtful silence. In my effort for quick answers, most of the time what leaped into my mind, came out of my mouth without much screening. Sometimes this worked. Often it didn't. Could it be that God was trying to teach me to think before speaking?

Several weeks later a new rule came down from the management concerning our store hours. Normally the store opened at 9 a.m. and closed at 9 p.m. The new idea was to stay open each night until 9:10 to accommodate shoppers who couldn't get there by 9. When I heard this, I thought it was someone's idea of a bad joke. Then I found out it was actually true. The store implemented the change and we started staying open until 9:10. A week later the district manager came by to see how things were going. I told him flat out I thought it was the stupidest idea I'd ever heard. I said, "O.K., so we stay open 'til 9:10 for the people who can't get here by 9. What's next? We stay open 'til 9:30 for the folks who can't get here by 9:10? What about the ones who can't get here by 9:30? Should we stay open 'til 10? At this rate we'll be open 24 hours a day. I think it's the most ridiculous thing I've heard." The district manager replied, "It was *my* idea, and if you don't like it you can find yourself another job."

The next thought that came into my head was, "I've got two words for you and one of them is off." I thought it – but I didn't say it. I actually kept quiet. I didn't say, "Yes, that's a great idea boss," because that would have been a lie. I just said nothing. Could it be I was finally learning to keep my big trap shut?

Several days later something else happened that made me wonder the same thing. I walked up to a customer and said, "Hi!" He looked right through me as if I wasn't there and did not speak. Ignoring this gesture, I made eye contact with him and cheerfully said, "Do you need help with anything?" He looked at me scornfully and said, "I wouldn't be *ignoring you* if I needed any help."

When I heard these words, I felt a rush of heat in my face. My ears felt hot. I was sure my blood pressure was at a critical level. I was also sure that if I said what I was thinking I would surely get fired. Once again I said nothing -- and walked away. I was finally learning to not speak my mind.

When I was in radio, everyone seemed so friendly. It was hard when I came down from my ivory tower and mingled with real people. As an "only child" with no brothers or sisters, I never really learned the concept of giving and sharing. I was just a loner, trying to survive by wits alone. It finally began to make sense. I had placed far too much emphasis on "being right" and not enough on "being right with God." I've learned I don't always have to be right. I don't have to be funny. I just have to ask God what he wants me to do in each situation. Then get quiet and listen.

Don Corey

It's simple. I didn't say it was easy.

For about a seven-year period I decided to try my hand at some other career besides sales. I took, and passed, the civil service test and began to work for the U.S. Government.

A woman named Eunice worked in the same office. She seemed like a nice person, but for some reason she fiercely disliked me. I did not know why -- as far as I knew I had never done anything to upset her. All the same, it was obvious that she despised me. I always try to get along with everyone, so I decided to do something about it.

I stopped by her desk one day and asked, "Eunice -- is there something I did that offended you?" She looked at me and said, "I don't like you. I don't want you coming around, I don't want to talk to you and I don't want you to talk to me. Just stay away from me and leave me alone." That pretty much summed it up. No mistaking it, she flat out didn't like me. I mumbled, "Uh, O.K. then," and made my exit.

Just that week I had read an interesting book about the power of prayer. Not prayer where you ask for yourself, but prayer for someone else. A secret prayer, no one knows about. I decided to try it.

My desk was at the front of the room, so Eunice had to pass by several times a day. Each time she passed by, I would think silently, "God Loves You." I did not tell anyone about this. It was not an attempt to alter the way she felt about me, I knew that was out of the question. It just seemed to me it couldn't do any harm

-- and everyone needs to know that God loves them.

I did this every day for a week. I never spoke to her, just prayed each time she passed by. A week later, she stopped right in front of my desk and said, "Don, you look nice today." I almost fell out of my chair! I quickly and simply said, "Thank you." She turned and walked away.

I'm not saying the two of us became the best of friends. But from then on, she was cordial to me and when we spoke to each other she was never rude again.

I knew I had witnessed a miracle. Try it and see for yourself. Don't tell anyone else. Just do it and see what happens.

SIXTEEN

About 1977 a girl named Linda invited me to attend her church service. I only went along to be polite, but it was actually a life altering experience.

I had always considered myself a fairly nice guy. Oh, I had some flaws and faults and a few bad habits -- but by and large, a pretty nice fellow, thank you very much.

God convinced me that night that instead I was broken beyond repair. At first, I was devastated. But then I received the good news, the gospel of the Christ. I never understood it before, but in that very moment it hit me. My life would never be the same.

I hoped I would suddenly change and discard all my faults and bad habits. It did not happen that way at all. But once God revealed Himself to me, I knew I couldn't go back to the way I was before.

I never really started living until I stopped being scared. I thought I was looking for answers, but like all of us, we're really looking for God. Believe me when I tell you, He's looking for you too. I still don't know exactly what He has in mind for my life, but I know He is always there and He never lets me down. I spent most of my life running after everything I thought was important, but in the end none of it satisfies that emptiness deep inside.

 If you already know God and Jesus personally, that's great. My job here is done. If you don't, you seriously need to make it your top priority. Don't kid yourself with those crazy "self improvement" schemes. You can spend the rest of your life trying to "fix yourself" and you will never get there. Ever. Don't wait until you hit rock bottom to figure this out. I challenge you: put as much effort into getting God into your life as you would anything else you've ever tried. It doesn't matter if you've failed or succeeded. If you succeeded at something, use that same zeal for God. If you've failed at something, that's even better. Take that failure, admit that you need some help, and let God help you. Don't waste another minute. You never know how much time you have left.

Each and every experience I've gone through in life has taught me two things. What I learned from the event, and what I learned about myself. I still have the Bible that I received as a small child. When I got it, I had just learned to write. Inside the front cover I wrote, "Don Corey the great."

I marveled at this later. Just how great can one be at that age? I had only just learned how to arrange letters to form words. This didn't exactly make me a child prodigy. I'm sure most people would conclude that this was clearly a case of an inferiority complex, which was being covered up with a superiority complex. I don't see it that way at all. This was God's way of telling me, even at that young age, that He created me. *Everything God creates is great.* It is only when we depart from his power that we become tarnished and imperfect.

When I met and married Katherine, I finally awakened to the fact that it really *is* more blessed to give than to receive. Prior to this I had always understood it as a nice concept, but difficult to put into practice. While believing the truth, I still tried to keep one foot in "giving," and the other one in "those who die with the most toys wins." Of course, intellectually I knew this would not fly. But it's hard to let go. Katherine demonstrated that this was not just possible -- she lived it. She is absolutely the most caring, giving person I have ever known and yet she doesn't feel that she's done anything special. She's just being herself.

Our lives together have seen many strange and amazing coincidences, over and over again. I never quite know what's coming next. I had spoken for years about writing a book but I never had the courage to do it until Katherine. She is very supportive of my ideas although I'm sure she's glad I finally put the lid on this one.

Originally I was going to title this book, "What ever

happened to what's his name?" I went through several changes but no matter what I came up with, it just didn't seem right. The last one I came up with was, "Any chance I could start over?" which Katherine disliked immensely. At last I said, out loud, "Well God, what do you want the title to be?" Within 30 seconds I had the answer. "Are you talking to me?"

This proved to me several things. First, God has a sense of humor. Second, He answers prayer when you're sincere. But most importantly it showed me that prayer is so much more than just asking for favors. God wants us to talk to Him. Not just for the big stuff, but the little stuff too.

I also want to acknowledge my closest and dearest friends, Steve Melton, Dave Roberts and Jon Liston. These guys always believed in me even when others did not. They are a constant source of inspiration and my life would not be what it is today without their influence.

Another person who changed my life for the better is my Junior High School science teacher, James Shackelford. School and I did not get along right from the start, but he had a unique style of teaching that brought me out of my rebellious shell and showed me that learning could be fun and rewarding.

So now it turns out I have all the wits I need. God supplies everything. Even if I ask the wrong questions, I know God has all the right answers if only I will listen.

God revealed to me that it was futile to try to understand him with my intellect.

Are You Talking To Me?

He said, "The reason you have trouble is that you cannot conceive anything that has no beginning and no end."

Amen.

Afterword

Two days before his death, my husband Don Corey said these words to me. "If anything happens to me before I finish proofing my book, you have to promise that you will see that it gets published". I laughed and mentioned what a morbid thing to say. He said it again and so I promised him. I guess the joke was on me. My husband died on October 21, 2007 from a sudden heart attack. We were just going to celebrate our 6th wedding anniversary.He made everyday of my life special. To honor him I kept my promise to make sure his book was published.

Katherine Corey.

Biography

Don Corey is a former disc jockey who has packed a lifetime of different adventures into a very short span of time. "Are You Talking To Me" represents a condensed version of a peculiar life ride filled with coincidence and serendipity. Besides radio announcing, Don has done stand-up comedy, motivational speaking, and has developed personalized audio and video productions for his clients. He lives with his wife, Katherine in St. Louis, Missouri.

Photo Credits

Photo	Taken by
Me & Dad	Lorraine Corey
Helen & Grandpa	Minnie Suerig
Bowling Side View	Don Corey
Bowling rear view	Don Corey
Dad, Mom, Helen, Grandpa	Don Corey
Great Grandma Minnie	Helen Shillito
Mom	Duane Corey
Homemade Radio Station	Dave Roberts
KSHE overhead view	Steve Melton

Don Corey

KSHE Side View

Steve Melton

Author back page picture

Prestige Portraits,
photographer
Jason Myers

Printed in the United States
126728LV00001B/135/A